THE LORD'S PRAYER

An esoteric Christian perspective

Adrian Anderson PhD

The insights of Rudolf Steiner affirmed by a fresh approach to the ancient Greek text of the Prayer

Distributed by Ebooks Alchemy
Prahran East
VIC 3198
Australia

© Copyright, 2025, Adrian Anderson
Threshold Publishing, Australia

All rights reserved

Cover image: courtesy of M. Swann

ISBN 9780645195460   paperback

Introduction 2

PART ONE
The seven pleas of the Prayer and 6
the sevenfold human nature

The opening words ('our Father') 11

What is the 'cosmic' Christ? 13

First plea: 'name be sanctified' 17

Second plea: 'kingdom draw near' 20

Third plea: 'Thy Will come into being' 20

Fourth plea: 'our bread' 22
   exploring the meaning of 'epiousion' 23
   What does 'mahar' mean? 31

Fifth plea: 'moral debts' 49
   forgiving sins, cancelling sinfulness

Sixth plea: 'not bring us into temptation' 64
   about God and evil

Seventh plea: 'draw us away from evil' 81

The entire Lord's Prayer 83

PART TWO
A: The prayer in Luke's Gospel 84

B: "Let Thy Holy Spirit come.." 91
   Marcion, Tertullian, Origenes, Gregory

C: The doxology (for Thine are the Power...) 103

Appendix 1: the 'i' left in epiousion 110
Appendix 2: the words formed for MHR 112
Appendix 3: three other versions 113

Books by this author 118

The Lord's Prayer: translated A. Anderson

Our Father, Thou in the Heavens,
Let Thy name be sanctified
Let Thy Kingdom draw near
Let Thy will come into being:
As in Heaven, so upon the Earth.
Give to us daily our bread:
'bread' above physical substance,
   which offers itself up to us.
And forgive us our moral debts,
   as we also forgive those who become
   indebted to us,
and, may Thou not bring us into temptation.
but draw us away from evil.

For Thine is the Power, the Kingdom and the Glory, forever and ever; amen.

The Lord's Prayer: the NIV version

Our Father in heaven
hallowed be your name,
your kingdom come,
your will be done,
on earth as it is in heaven.
Give us today our daily bread
And forgive us our debts,
as we also have forgiven our debtors.
And lead us not into temptation,
but deliver us from the evil one.

INTRODUCTION

The Lord's Prayer has been profoundly revered for 2,000 years as the holy core text of Christianity, inspiring many hundreds of millions of souls. All of chapters 5, 6 and 7 in Matthew's Gospel are filled with the teachings of the Saviour. It is in the midst of this extensive narrative that the Lord's Prayer is presented; in chapter 6: 9-13.

My contemplations on this Prayer have as their basis, an 'esoteric' perspective on Christianity namely that there is a cosmic dimension to 'Christ'. This perspective yields a deeper and broader understanding of the Prayer than is usually achieved. This perspective is not an arbitrary one; many aspects of it can be validated from the Greek text of the Gospels.

This cosmic view of Christ is found in the teachings of Origenes of Alexandria. This 'cosmic' dimension to the Lord's Prayer is clearly presented in the work of Rudolf Steiner, and it is also presented in the Gospels, but in these it is veiled. I have endeavoured to engage with these perspectives through an academically rigorous assessment of the ancient Greek texts of the Gospels.

The Lord's Prayer, although quite short and devoid of complex language, has an immensely deep esoteric meaning. It was also proclaimed within a religious-spiritual context which was itself underpinned by an initiatory quest, amongst both the Hebrew and Grecian cultures of the Hellenistic Age.

The primary facet in a cosmic view of Christianity is that the word 'Christ' refers to a divine being, a deity, who is distinct from the man Jesus, although this sublime deity became united with Jesus (see below).

In the first three centuries of the church, there existed an esoteric or initiatory Christianity; this is affirmed by various ancient documents. But by the fourth century this wonderful aspect of Christianity faded out. Since then this is regarded as an invalid, unsubstantiated fantasy. But there is substantial evidence in the Gospel texts themselves that supports this esoteric view. Some of this evidence will be considered here. My *The Gospel of John*, presents a detailed consideration of the evidence. Here I shall briefly mention the ancient Coptic Pistis Sophia codex which preserves a large body of teachings which – excluding the last two texts of this compilation of various documents – derive from the risen Jesus. There is also the document found in Mt. Sinai – a letter from Clement of Alexandria to a student which specifically refers to a secret gospel of St. Mark.[1] There are also other comments from Clement in his 'Stromaties', and from his student the great Origenes, which indicate that an esoteric Christianity existed discretely alongside of the mainstream church. Moreover, in the Book of Revelation many deeply esoteric matters to do with the initiatory path are presented, although veiled.

Rudolf Steiner asserted that the 'Father' to whom the Prayer is dedicated, is the cosmic Christ; this topic is discussed below. Before considering the theme of the Father being, in this context, the 'cosmic Christ', we need to consider the nature of Christ.

---

[1] It was discovered by Prof. M. Smith, and published in *Clement of Alexandria and a Secret Gospel of St. Mark*, (1973, Harvard UP). Unfortunately scholars other than the discoverer, have never been able to see the original letter, and its whereabouts is unknown, as all attempts to find it have been unsuccessful.

In an initiatory understanding of Christianity, Jesus is a member of the human live-wave, although indeed the holiest of all humans. But through the Baptism in the Jordan river, and through the events on Golgotha hill, a sublime deity, the 'cosmic Christ', permeated the being of Jesus; thereby bringing fully into existence 'Jesus Christ'.

In the writings of Origenes and of Rudolf Steiner, 'Christ' is presented as the highest of the deities known as the Powers (or in Greek, Exousiai) in the language of St. Paul. However, there is a still higher aspect to Christ, when the term 'Christ' is applied to the Logos, who is a sublime deity in the triune Godhead. (See below for more about this.)

To comprehend the deeper meaning of the Prayer, Rudolf Steiner's explanation of the structure of the cosmos, and the structure of the human being's soul and spirit, is very helpful. Both of these realities have a sevenfold nature, and these two are intimately interwoven. This view is an essential help in grasping the deeper message of the Gospels; see diagram.

The 7 pleas in the Lord's Prayer

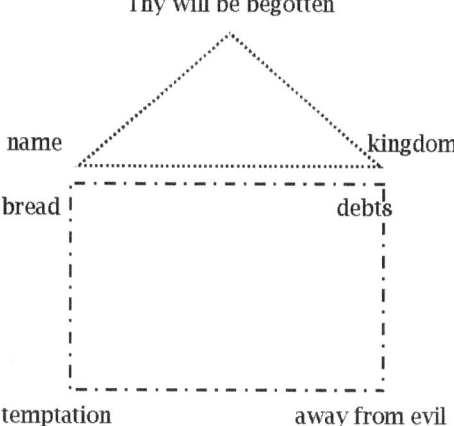

The 7-fold human being

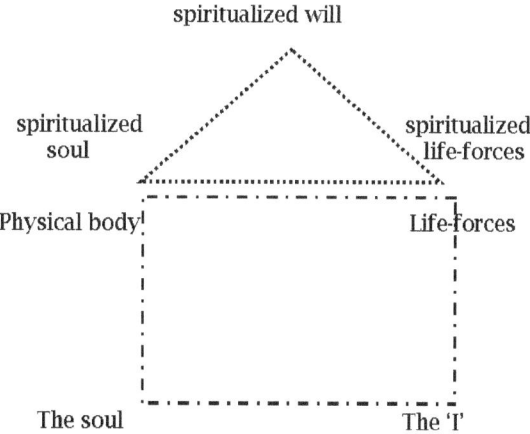

This diagram is adapted from Rudolf Steiner's graphics in a lecture of 28th Jan. 1907 (bk. No, 96)

Diagram of the dual sevenfoldness

The sevenfold nature of the Prayer and of human nature.
The seven specific pleas or petitions in the Prayer were given by Christ to correlate to the over-all structure of the human being. The idea that our human nature has seven aspects to it is at first puzzling, but this is resolved when the concept is carefully considered.

1: the physical-flesh body: in the world-view presented by Rudolf Steiner the physical body is viewed as a marvel of wisdom, with systems or functions incorporated into it, as developed over vast Ages, that allow the human soul to manifest its capacity for thinking, for emotions and of will.

2: our life-forces or ethereal energies; these are known in China as 'Ch'i and in India as 'prana'. This is known as the 'etheric-body' in Steiner's work. The etheric body is a definable, gently glowing organism made of four kinds of energies which are more subtle than those of the electromagnetic spectrum. It is this which keeps the physical body alive. It has approximately the shape of our physical body, but it extends beyond the body, only a half inch or so, except at some points such as the finger-tips, from where it rays out a short distance.

3: the soul: the soul appears to clairvoyant vision as the well-known 'aura', which is an oval shape of living colour-forms, surrounding our physical body and etheric bodies. The aura is like an egg-shaped glow surrounding us. It extends about a metre below our feet and above our head, and on all sides around us.

The soul or soul-body comprises our feelings, our intelligence and our Will or volitional powers. This soul-organism, or 'soul-body' is called the 'soul body' or 'astral-body' in Steiner's works.

Within itself our soul has three components; namely emotions, intellect and will. This triune nature was perceived by the religious leaders of ancient civilisations. In Hebrew, there are the terms, Nephesch, Ruach and Neschamah, each referring to a different soul dynamic.

Likewise in ancient Greece, there is the Orektikon, Kinektikon and Dionetikon. In ancient Egypt, amongst a variety of terms, there are the words Kha(ba), Akhu and Putah for these three components.

4: the 'I' or sense of self. It is this fourth member of our human nature which is our 'self-awareness'; the awareness that we are a separate entity. The term 'ego' is used in anthroposophical literature for this aspect of our nature, and means the sense of our own individuated being-ness; it is not a pejorative term. To make this quite clear to his students, Steiner often used the term "I" (in German the word, "Ich") rather than 'ego'.

This fourth aspect, our 'I', is actually a very complex and subtle part of our being. This is discussed in my *Rudolf Steiner Handbook*.

With this fourth member of our nature, the 'fourfold human being has been presented. The next aspects, the 5th, 6th and 7th, are present only in a germinal form in the normal person. These three next aspects are of a divine or spiritual nature.

5: the Spiritual-self or spiritualized, i.e., sanctified, soul. When the three elements of our personality, that is, our soul, is spiritualized then the purity of the desires, the wisdom permeating the intelligence and selflessness in the will, brings into being the first of our triune spiritual reality: the Spiritual-self.

6: The Life-spirit: this can also be called the 'spiritualized life-forces' (etheric body); this occurs when the now purified soul allows the life-forces to become imbued with divine energies. One becomes an empowered person, able to move beyond what could be called 'passive' compassion to active compassion. That is, when this stage of sanctification is attained, a higher consciousness arises giving perception of divine realities. In addition, healing of sick people or creating exquisitely beautiful and deeply meaningful art becomes a capacity.

7: the Spirit-human: this stage is reached when the divine energies present, but deeply veiled, in the physical body are raised to consciousness. These energies are closely related to our Will, and to divine Will. This seventh aspect of our nature arises when these veiled Will qualities are integrated into the now highly enlightened consciousness.

So the first three pleas are about the triune human spiritual potential, whilst each of the four lower pleas relates to one of the four lower aspects of the human being. Hence, the first three pleas of the Lord's Prayer concern divine realities; whilst the next four pleas concern very much the earthly human being.

The reader may not be aware that one of the pleas in this Prayer has a Greek word which no scholar has ever been able to fully understand; this word is unique in all ancient Greek literature, and therefore scholars have been unable to agree as to what it actually means. This word is 'epiousion' and it occurs in the plea, "Give us this day our daily bread."

Several different meanings have been suggested, but there is no universally agreed-upon meaning; and so the word 'daily' has been put into the verse. Therefore one may say that this verse has never been correctly translated in any version of the Bible.

However, I conclude that my research into this word has unveiled what it means. So in this book, I am presenting the results of my engagement with this enigmatic ancient Greek word of Matthew's Gospel. This allows a more profound understanding of the petition about the daily bread.

But there is another important outcome of my work here, which may be a new contribution to the research undertaken into the Prayer. For some of the original Hebrew text of Matthew's Hebrew-language Gospel has survived, but it appears that investigation into the Hebrew adjective in this text about 'bread' has seldom been undertaken.[2]

Furthermore, the most comprehensive Biblical Hebrew dictionary is seldom consulted, as it has been out of print for about 130 years (although a scanned photocopy of this German text is now accessible). This old text makes possible much more informed research into such words. (More about this resource later.)

A primary feature of my work was to contemplate the Prayer from the perspective of it having a seven-fold structure: three higher pleas and then four less transcendent pleas. It is in the lectures of Rudolf Steiner that one learns that this structure

---

[2] Professor Lux, in his large 3-vol. study of Matthew's Gospel (*Das Evangelium nach Matthäus*) references some 120 commentaries and 90 essays on this Gospel – without any indication that this Hebrew word was ever investigated.

correlates to the above presented sevenfold structure of the human being.

Contemplating the Lord's Prayer
My work on this Prayer involved a careful assessment of academic commentaries on the Greek text by leading Bible scholars. But these Commentaries lack awareness that the key to engaging with this Prayer is to realize that the teachings given in the three chapters of Matthew's Gospel in which this Prayer is given, only occurred after Jesus "went up the mountain".

Before this event, he had contemplated crowds of people with higher consciousness (clairvoyance):

Chapter 5:1 "Then, when Jesus had gazed spiritually at the crowds, he went up on a mountainside and sat down. His disciples came to him, and he began to teach them...."

The expression 'to go up on the mountain' is a veiled esoteric term intended to let the spiritually informed reader know that the Teacher has raised his consciousness to the spiritual realms, beyond sense-perception.

When Christ was teaching his disciples, he did at times raise his clairvoyance up into higher spiritual realms (referred to as 'Devachan'). From there he would, with the 12 Disciples, intone sublime truths. In the case of the Transfiguration, he took just three Disciples with him.

At other times, the Gospel writer, inspired by the risen Jesus to see these events in visionary form, could record that many not-incarnate human spirits were witnesses to Christ in higher realms. This presence of people not in the physical bodies, is recorded for example, in Matthew's Gospel at the end of the three chapters of exalted teachings (7:28-9), in which the Lord's Prayer was given.

First references to the Prayer outside the Gospel of Matthew

This prayer was included in a very early Christian theological text called 'The Teachings' ('the Didache' in Greek); a document which is hard to date, estimates vary from AD 50 to AD 80.

The Prayer was also included in the 'Diatessaron', written about AD 150 by Tatian, an Assyrian Christian writer (he lived approx. AD 110-171). His text was an ill-advised attempt to produce a 'harmony' of the four Gospels in one 'smoothed-out' Gospel, in which 'discrepancies' between the accounts were harmonized.

Among the some significant new perspectives about this Prayer that this book shall be presenting, is the view that the Lord's Prayer is not in fact also recorded in the Gospel of Luke (11:2-4). Luke's Gospel presents a prayer which does contain some of the verses in the Lord's Prayer, but it is a different prayer, with a different intention. This theme is discussed in detail in Part Two of this book.

The opening words: 'our Father….'

It is striking that God is addressed as 'Father', for this was not a common practice amongst the ancient Hebrews. But it harmonizes with the various references to God in the teachings of Jesus in the Gospels. The ancient Hebrews themselves seldom referred to 'God' as their personal 'Father'. For if God was described as a 'father', then he was the father of their nation.

In the Hebrew Bible, this occurs only in Isaiah (63:14), Deuteronomy (32:6) and possibly in Psalm 103:13. However it is present in a few later Hebrew texts in the Apocrypha, e.g., Wisdom 2:16 and Tobit 13:4. When contemplating these esoteric themes, it is more natural for us to consider the cosmic Christ as 'creator' rather than 'father'; yet the Prayer quite intentionally teaches us to understand him as 'father'.

The term 'God' is actually a vague term, and consequently it is used in many different ways, and in fact implies or refers to different deities. From Rudolf Steiner's lectures on Biblical themes, and from a study of the Hebrew words of the Old Testament for 'God', one learns that the term 'God' can have a variety of meanings in Biblical texts, although this is not so obvious in an English translation.

In the Book of Genesis there are references to 'the Elohim', which are a group of deities viewed in Rudolf Steiner's research as 'the Powers'. Jahve is one of these deities; he is traditionally called 'the Lord God' in Bibles.

But there is also the triune Godhead, in which 'God' refers to the highest of these three, often called the 'Weltengrund'. However, the highest deity amongst the Elohim is that deity known in esoteric Christianity as 'the cosmic Christ'.

Hence if by 'Father' a Scriptural text means 'God', as here in the Lord's Prayer, it follows that 'Father' also is a term with several possible meanings; it can refer to several deities. As noted earlier, Rudolf Steiner taught that in the Lord's Prayer 'Father' refers to the cosmic Christ, the leader of the Powers, and thus not to the 'Weltengrund' for example. That is, it does not refer to the primal God in the triune Godhead, who is above the nine ranks of 'hierarchical' spirits.[3]

This perspective that the cosmic Christ is called 'the Father,' may at first appear odd, until one

---

[3] This is presented in Complete Works no. 343, p.194.

recalls that the *Book of Genesis* portrays the Elohim (the leader of whom is the cosmic Christ) as the Creator (and thus the 'Father') of humanity. So it is quite feasible to view the cosmic Christ as the 'Father' of humanity.

This conclusion about the 'Father' is further affirmed by the sublime events in the *Book of Exodus* (chap. 3) when Moses encounters the burning bush, and enquires as the name of the Deity who addresses him from the bush.

As I have presented in detail elsewhere, the name of God which was then given to Moses, is in effect, " I am the '*I am*' ", meaning:

"I, JHVH-Christ, am the innermost 'I' in you"; in other words, I am your self-sense, or your 'I am' – that is, once your self, your consciousness, has been spiritualized.[4]

So from this, one may consider Jahve-Christ to be 'our Father'; a conclusion which is affirmed by that very specific addition to the Lord's Prayer: "As in Heaven, so upon the Earth". For this focus upon the Earth becoming a place where divine reality is actively present, is central to the deeds of Jesus and mission of Christ.

What is the cosmic Christ?

In esoteric Christian knowledge, the Powers are regarded as the same as the deities called Elohim in the Hebrew Scriptures. These are understood to be deities whose 'location' is in the 'Sun-sphere'. Thus Christ is understood as the 'Sun-god Christ'; that is, the leading deity in the Sun-sphere – in the sense of the 'planetary spheres' of the ancient Ptolemaic solar system. What evidence is there for this conclusion?

---

[4] This theme is discussed in my *Rudolf Steiner's esoteric Christianity in the Grail Painting by Anna May.*

There are nine ranks of divine beings known to those on the initiatory path in the Hellenistic world, both Hebrews and early Christians. When the list of these deities is placed onto the Ptolemaic planetary spheres, the Powers have the Sun-sphere as their location. They are the fourth rank of deities, after the Angels (Moon), the Archangels (Venus) and the Principalities (Mercury).

Although mainstream theology ignores this more 'holistic' or directly spiritual aspect to the Christian context, an ancient Christian document has survived which describes these nine ranks of deities. This is the very old *'Testament of Adam'* which dates from the second century CE.

This priceless text is almost unknown, as it is rarely included in theological studies. The knowledge of these same nine ranks of beings is also recorded in the writings of Dionysius the Areopagite; he lived in the 1st century CE, and became a pupil of St. Paul. But his teachings have only survived in a fifth century document.

Is the cosmic Christ a Power?
Are the Powers really the same deities as the Elohim, that is, the group of deities who created our world, as presented in Chapter One of Genesis? If so, then Christ, as the highest of the Powers, is a Sun-deity.

Since the esoteric truths, with their more confronting cosmic nature were kept private, there are no direct statements in the Hebrew Scriptures identifying the Elohim as from the Sun-sphere.

However, such deeper truths are less veiled in some places in Scripture. One such example is in the book of the Psalms; many deep initiatory truths are to be found in them. Psalm 19 is especially relevant here, as it directly implies that Yahweh, and thereby also Christ, are deities whose location is in the Sun-sphere. This Psalm begins with a reference to a wonderful esoteric theme: the interconnectedness of the human being and the planetary system.

The first section of the beautifully poetic Psalm 19 is actually about the planetary spheres, and the core spiritual truth that human language arises from the influence of the planets resonating within the soul-body.

It is the last line which is so important regarding the Sun; it refers to the planets of our solar system. It is often translated as:

"In them he has set a tabernacle for the Sun".

But there are two small prefixes in the Hebrew text, which mean 'among' (בְּ) or 'in' (לְ), etc. So the last line can also fully validly be translated as:
"*Among* them he has set his tabernacle *in* the Sun."
This is a remarkable statement, which specifically places the location of 'God' (i.e., JHVH-Christ) in the Sun-sphere, in the midst of the planets. This is not an invalid interpretation which disregards the grammar and the context; this is how Jewish scholars themselves long ago understood the text, when they translated the Hebrew text into Greek, in the Septuagint some centuries before the time of Jesus :
       "He put his tabernacle in the Sun".[5]

This then is my translation of the beginning of the Psalm:

>The Heavens* declare the glory of God,
>(*planetary spheres)
>And the Firmament reveals his efficacy,

---

[5] Septuagint Ps. 18, v. 4 : ἐν τῷ ἡλίῳ ἔθετο τὸ σκήνωμα αὐτοῦ.

> For speech arises from within each day,
> And inner knowing arises from within each night.
> There is no speech, nor language, where the voice of the planetary spheres is not heard.
> And their resonance encompasses all the globe;
> Among these influences, God has set up his tabernacle in the Sun.[6]

So here is strong support for identifying the Elohim as divine beings whose location is in the Sun-sphere; that is, the Elohim who were later known to the Greeks as the 'Powers'. That the esoteric message here is somewhat veiled is to be expected. This because the Hebrew people were not to be focused on the cosmos, and thereby revere planetary deities. They were to focus on their own inner nature, and how the commands of God should be resonating in their souls.

Another text which identifies the Christ as a Power, and hence located in the Sun-sphere is in the work of the great Origenes of Alexandria. It is in his *Commentary on the Gospel of John*, (para. 291-92),

> For frequently (*in Scripture*) it is set forth, "For thus says 'the Lord of the Powers' (or, Lord of *Spirit Hosts*)".[7] This phrase refers to certain individuated beings: spirits high and divine, who are designated "Powers" – of whom Christ (*the solar Logos*) was the highest and the finest.

---

[6] In the Septuagint: 'in the Sun' = ἐν τῷ ἡλίῳ

[7] In the Hebrew Scriptures or Old Testament, God is sometimes called in Hebrew, 'Yahweh who has an army or host of powerful spirits'. But only once (in the Septuagint) is the version, the "Lord of Powers" used (at 2Kgs. 19:20).

This very important teaching, revealing the cosmic nature of Christianity, as known to those who shared in esoteric Christian knowledge of antiquity, has been neglected by scholars. This is partly due to the fact that these words occur in a grammatically difficult section in Origenes' ancient Greek. These paragraphs are explored in detail in my translation and commentary of them, in my *The Gospel of John.*

In this view, the words of Jesus are experienced as often being intoned by the sublime Christ-being. Although in traditional translations the group of Elohim who brought forth the solar system at 'the Beginning' are referred to in the singular as 'God'; but in esoteric Christianity, this view of the Elohim as a singular deity is understood to be an error.

FIRST PLEA: **Let Thy name be sanctified**
correlates to: the Spiritual-self

As with all these pleas or petitions, the entreaty is being directed to 'God', understood here as the cosmic Christ. Now, on the exoteric cultural level, this entreaty is asking that people feel reverence for the Father (in whatever way that word may be understood). In religious contexts, any use of the word 'God' (or 'the Father') in church or in religious conversations, will be regarded as referring to a sacred, or sanctified, divine being.

So, when the word Father (or God) is used in this Prayer, people will feel reverence. However, neither 'God' nor 'Father' is actually a name, these two words are really titles of a deity. So any deeper discussion of the theme of God's 'name' raises the question of, what is the actual name of 'the Father'? In exoteric or humanistic theology, this question remains a sacred enigma, a riddle which cannot be answered. For this reason the ancient

Hebrews regarded the actual name of God as something too holy to pronounce, hence it remained unknown to all but a few.

A version of the name which humans were permitted to pronounce, was created by the Hebrew priesthood. But only their High Priest was permitted to pronounce this name, and then only once a year, within the Holy of Holies.

To those on the initiatory path, the above question becomes deepened and extraordinarily relevant. For Rudolf Steiner revealed that as initiatory consciousness develops, the person develops their higher qualities or their 'Spiritual-self'. In anthroposophical knowledge, this state is understood to be what is meant by the Biblical phrase 'The Son of Man' - when it is not directly referring to Jesus himself.

Now, to the person on the initiatory path, a deeply felt immensely transformative experience occurs. When this high spiritual stage of the Spiritual-self is reached, then one's own name changes. Or rather, one begins to perceive that holiness is present in one's now spiritualized soul. This appears to require another name, not the name which is identifiable with one's earthly nature.

This new-born part of one's being has its own name; a word or 'intoning' which is deeply sacred and private. It is this same situation which is directly, if discreetly, announced in the Book of Revelation, when it is referring to becoming initiated;

Rev. 2:17 "Whoever has ears, let them hear what the Spirit says to the churches. To the one who is victorious (*on the initiatory path*), I will give to eat of the hidden manna. I shall also give that person a transparent shining crystal, with a new name written on it; (a name) known only to the one who receives it."   (trans. the author)

Rudolf Steiner explains that the person on the initiatory quest perceives that this new name – which represents a holy, higher aspect of one's being – is in fact derived from a divine source; from our Creator, or Father; that is, the cosmic Christ.

Our own new, secret name is in effect, the result of a ray of light from the Divine, from the cosmic Christ, permeating one's soul, and mightily developing our incipient spiritual nature (or spirit-aura[8]); hence it is through this process that the name of 'the Father' – which is the new name one senses in one's own inner nature – becomes sanctified. The earnest prayer of any person on the Christian initiatory path is for this sublime experience to be attained.

This is what Steiner, as the great teacher of the initiatory Christian Mysteries, has presented on this subject; or rather it is one of two revelations from him. It could be called 'the path to the Divine within'. For Rudolf Steiner gave another revelation about the petition, 'Let thy name become sanctified'; this other revelation is 'the path to the Divine above and without'. As he taught a small group when referring to this plea,

"Behold the things around you: these, in their great diversity, are an expression of Deity ! If you speak their (*veiled, spiritual*) names, then you have comprehended them as aspects of the divine world-order. What you may have in your environs, is to be regarded as holy. And within the name which you give to all these things, perceive something which confirms that it is a part of Divine Being-ness."[9]

It is clear, that to achieve this inner knowing of the

---

[8] A higher reality than the soul-aura or soul-body.
[9] In book no. 96, lect. of 28th Jan. 1907.

core quality of the creatures and plants in Nature requires a high degree of spiritual consciousness.

SECOND PLEA:
Let thy kingdom draw near
correlates to: the spiritualized life-forces

We have just seen how immensely deep and inspiring is Rudolf Steiner's initiatory understanding of the first plea. The second and third pleas concern even higher, more potent truths; but these thereby transcend our capacity to grasp. So we can be given little more than a silhouette of what they actually mean.

The second plea about the kingdom drawing near, is connected with the development of one's 'Life-spirit'; this part of the sevenfold human being arises as the life-forces (or the 'etheric body') becomes freed from sensuality, and becomes highly spiritualized. When this stage is attained, one's life-energies are in complete harmony with the Divine.

THIRD PLEA:
Let thy Will come into being (or, 'be begotten').
correlates to: the spiritualized Will

This plea concerns the releasing of our will from the impact of the physical matter in our body, and also from even the most subtle egotistical intentions. So one is free from intentions focused solely upon the material world; and one is also freed from any anti-social, self-centred intentions.

The will then has a loving, self-sacrificing quality, echoing the selflessness of the Father God when he put into reality his intention to create the universe.[10] The following words from Rudolf Steiner about the nature of God are from his own experiential insights – derived from his initiatory consciousness and meditation on this theme –

> "The Weltengrund (God) has fully poured out Himself into the cosmos. He has not withdrawn from it in order to guide it from outside. Rather He impels it from within; so He has not withheld Himself from it. The highest mode of His manifestation within the reality of normal existence is (human) thinking (*i.e., consciousness*) and through this factor, the human personality.
>
> Thus if God has goals, then they are identical with the (*moral*) goals that human beings set for themselves, for He lives within these. But this does not occur through the human being trying to investigate one or other command from this Regent of the cosmos, and acting according to such a perceived goal.
>
> It – the active involvement of God – occurs through the human being, acting from his or her own understanding. For this Regent of the Cosmos is living within these human beings. He does not exist as Will somewhere outside of the human being for he has forgone such a Will of his own, in order to make everything dependent upon the Will of the human being." [11]

Comment 1: 'the (*moral*) goals': I have added the word 'moral' as this appears to be what is meant.

---

[10] Rudolf Steiner has indicated that this means our galaxy.

[11] "Outlines of a theory of epistemology of the Goethean world-view" page 125 (German edition), in the chapter, *Human freedom.*

That is, as people set a moral goal – which may be far removed from a truly high spiritual ethic – God is subtly present within this effort, even if only in a weakly reflected way.

Comment 2: how does this description of God relate to the fervent prayer, "Not my will, but Thine be done". Although this was said by Jesus in the garden of Gethsemane, it became a prayer used by many Christians when facing serious difficulties in life.

In such a situation, the person is sensing that the Divine (or 'God') needs to be specifically entreated to become the primary reality in his or her will. In this way, the underlying impetus in our will for some pending decision, comes from the Divine – in a more empowered dynamic than its usual muffled presence.

So the third plea, "Let Thy Will come into being" is asking that our own will becomes so sanctified, that the selfless or self-sacrificing quality of God permeates our own intentions.

The four lower pleas
The Prayer now focuses on the four lower aspects of human nature: the physical body, the life-forces, the soul and the 'I'.

FOURTH PLEA:
Correlates to: the physical body

Give to us daily our bread; the 'bread' which is higher than physical substance, which offers itself up to us. (Matthew 6:11)

But, a common translation, as recited and used in prayer for millennia, is:
           "Give us today our daily bread",[12]

---

[12] In Greek, τὸν ἄρτον ἡμῶν τὸν ἐπιούσιον δὸς ἡμῖν σήμερον

However, the usual version, 'daily' is regarded by many scholars as an inaccurate presentation of the words of Christ. For as noted earlier, no agreement has been reached amongst scholars as to the meaning of one word in the prayer. This word is 'epiousion' (ἐπιούσιον) which is translated as either 'daily', or 'for tomorrow', or 'of necessity', for scholars struggle to interpret it, because it is unique to the Gospel.

Understanding 'epiousion'
This word is not found in any other ancient Greek text. In this section, I offer what I believe to be the actual meaning of this word in the Prayer. Various other interpretations exist. These include 'bread above all {other} things', 'bread according to our need'. A few scholars, including the great Origenes, have come nearer to what is meant, with 'higher or spiritual nourishment'.

However Origenes' view of this word was complex; in his essay "On Prayer', he writes of it as meaning 'needful', yet still having, as its prime meaning, nourishment which is above material substances.

Through the esoterically informed Initiatory Quest approach to Biblical interpretation, which I used for my translation of the Gospel of John, it is possible to ascertain the meaning of this unique Greek word, and thus of this verse in the Lord's Prayer. My research owes much to the work of Rudolf Steiner, but also to a meditative approach to Scripture, as well as a wider perspective on the Greek and Hebrew text of this verse, which opened up new avenues of research.

The enigmatic Greek term 'epiousion' has two components; epi (ἐπὶ) which generally means 'across' or 'above'; and ousias (οὐσιας) - it is this second part of the word which is so confusing. Although it is often interpreted to mean 'tomorrow' or 'daily', Origenes and other scholars conclude that it refers to 'substance' or 'essence'.

I hope to show that it is this interpretation which comes closest to the truth. We shall briefly survey the other interpretations, then focus on this word as meaning 'substance' or 'essence'.

1: 'daily' or 'for today': this is unconvincing for the substantial reason that the Greek language already has a word for this. So there was no need to create a new word which would puzzle the reader, preventing him or her from grasping what Christ is teaching in this verse.

2: 'bread of necessity' or 'needed bread': as with meaning One, this is unconvincing for the reason that the Greek language already has a word for this idea. There was no need to create another word, especially one which is so unclear as to its meaning, and hence would be enigmatic to most people.

3: 'for the future' (i.e., meaning divine soul-nutrition in a future Age): as with meanings One and Two, this is unconvincing again for the reason that the Greek language already has a word for this. So there was no purpose in creating a word that confronts the reader as an enigma.

4: 'bread for tomorrow' or 'for the coming day': these are grammatically and logically quite feasible, and are derived from a Greek term 'epeimi' (ἐπειμι) which means 'to approach' or 'to come near'. But this interpretation has the problem that if it were asking that we have enough food for tomorrow, it would be oriented to a much less profound level than the other petitions, as we shall see. So what does this mysterious word mean?

Exploring the meaning of epiousion

Firstly, 'epi' not only means 'above' or 'across', it also means, especially in Classical Greek, 'having authority over', or 'being superior to' (see below). And 'ousias' which in common Greek means 'property' or 'wealth', has other, more philosophical meanings in Classical Greek; namely 'substance' or essence.[13] It is by joining the two words and using their Classical Greek meanings that the meaning of epiousion emerges. Classical Greek terms are common in the New Testament.

However, there was a major objection from scholars to such a proposal, namely that 'epiousion' cannot be formed by joining these two words. This is because, according to the laws of Greek grammar, the 'i' from epi has to be dropped before the letter 'o' (making such a word theoretically: 'epousion'). This view has exerted enormous influence for many centuries: but in fact it is now conclusively shown to be a false argument.

Epiousion: that the 'i' can in fact be left in

Various scholars have argued that the joining of these two words, with the 'i' still retained, is permissible and has happened, even if strictly speaking, it should not retain the 'i'. Recent extensive scholarly research into this question, designed to resolve this enigma, discovered 26 examples of such compound words being formed in ancient Greek literature – despite the grammatical rule that the 'i' should be dropped.

---

[13] Nouns ending in 'ia' usually form their adjective as αιος or ώδης, but there are exceptions; for example, ἀνούσιος is used by Clement of Alexandria. So *ousia* **can** become ousios/ousion.

This scholar was a French cleric, J. Carmignac (1914-1986)[14]; his achievement is formally noted in the *Theological Lexicon of the New Testament*, edited by Ceslas Spicq. See Appendix One for more about this.

Before exploring 'epiousion' further in the light of Initiatory Quest insights, it is important to note the difficulty that humanistic theology has had in interpreting many words in the Gospels. It has doubted the presence of any deeper, more philosophical, or esoteric Classical Greek meanings in Gospel texts, as well as any esoteric teachings.

The Gospel message had to be simple and unsophisticated. This error is now being slowly corrected, with scholars showing the wide-spread prevalence of Classical Greek in the New Testament.

But still today, there lingers a major argument against accepting 'epiousion' as the result of joining epi and ousion. Namely, that the very concept that some subtle nutrient is being prayed for, which is superior to our body's substances, is not acceptable. This is because it is seen as too profound, too deep, for the 'simple' Lord's Prayer.

Comments expressing this view include:
"It belongs to a much later theological terminology, and is (thus) foreign to the simplicity of the Lord's Prayer";[15] "it is most improbable in a context so simple and direct as the Lord's Prayer"[16];

---

[14] In his "*Recherches sur le Notre Pere*", 1969.
[15] A. Carr, *The Gospel according to St. Matthew*, p. 129 Cambridge Univ, 1894.

[16] J. Moulton, *Grammar of NT Greek*, Vol. 2, T & T Clark, 1928, p. 313.

"Obviously 'ousia' in the sense of 'existence' or (physical) being cannot be confirmed as occurring in common usage", G. Kittel.[17]

My perspective is that the common view that the Prayer cannot have an initiatory, but veiled meaning, is displaying a sad lack of awareness of the immensely deep, even cosmic, perspectives that exist in the Gospels, which are often hidden behind apparently simple parables of Jesus. Hence more sophisticated words can be used.

However, there is a valid objection to interpreting 'epiousion' as meaning some subtle nourishment above material substance. This is when the interpretation is applied to the 'spiritual energy' which permeates the sanctified bread (or wine) used in the Eucharist or Mass. This view is primarily defended by Catholic scholars.

But as Lux comments, "…it imports later concepts into the passage and (so) does not fit the context well".[18] With these words Lux rightly comments it is impossible for epiousion to refer to the divine-spiritual presence of Christ within the sanctified wafer or wine used in the Mass or Eucharist, because such a refined theological concept 'belongs to a later age' than that of the Disciples.[19]

Rudolf Steiner pointed out that the Lord's Prayer is an immensely deep and complex text, because of the 'cosmic' dimension given to it from the Christ. It is precisely this missing cosmic dimension to

---

[17] *Theologisches Wörterbuch zum Neuen Testament* Vol. 2. In the German: Freilich ist 'ousia' in der Bedeutung, 'Dasein', 'Existenz' nicht als volkstümlich zu belegen.

[18] D. Hagner, *Matthew 1-13*, Word Books, 1993, p.149.

[19] U. Lux, *Das Evangelium nach Matthäus*, Vol.1. p.345, EKK, 1989.

Christianity in theology that weakens so much of the theological approach to Gospel passages.

We have noted that epi can mean 'having authority over', or 'being of a superior quality'; and ousias in Classical Greek also meant 'essence' or 'substance'. So it is a valid step to conclude, that epiousion means: 'having authority over substance', or 'nutrition higher than physical substance'. It is here that the correlation of the sevenfold Prayer to the sevenfold human being is able to give the key to understanding the word 'epiousion'. This verse is about our flesh body, so 'substance' refers to the substance of this body.

But there is still one more step to go, to unveil the real meaning of 'ousias'. Origenes saw epiousion as meaning 'above (our) substance', (in *On Prayer,* para. 7). A similar conclusion was reached by Jerome, for when he translated the Gospel of Luke from its Greek version into Latin, he translated 'epiousion' as 'supersubstantialis'.

Strangely, this word is generally defined in Latin dictionaries incorrectly as 'life-giving', for this is factually incorrect. It actually means 'above or superior to (one's) essence' or '(one's) substance'. Such a mysterious energy or subtle substance may well contribute to us staying alive, but not necessarily be generating life itself. Instead it may enhance, in a subtle way, the quality of the body.

So 'life-giving' is only one of several possible implications; it is actually only a derivative or secondary meaning.[20] In his *Commentary on St.*

---

[20] Tholuck (*Exposition of the Sermon on the Mount*, p.352) observes that 'epiousion' cannot be viewed as 'super-substantialis' (or überwesentlich in German); i.e., "above the natural bread", because 'huper' (ὑπέρ) should have been used, thus 'huperousiov'. And in fact Dionysos the Areopagite does use huperousiov (ὑπέρούσιος) in "*The*

Matthew Gospel (6:11) Jerome himself commented that, "We can understand 'supersubstantialis bread' as bread that is above all substances and surpasses all creatures."

So Jerome, like Origenes, understood epiousion as meaning 'higher than substance' or 'above substance'. But, not intuiting the correlation of this verse in the Prayer to our bodily nature, they thought it might refer to the spiritual presence of Christ, as in the wafer of bread in the Eucharist – however, that is not what is meant.

As noted earlier, it refers to a subtle nutrient which is superior to the physical substance of our body. But, because of the nature of theology, the more spiritually oriented or holistic explanation of epiousion was gradually rejected in favour of the now widely used superficial interpretation, 'daily' bread.

In addition to the other objections noted above to this interpretation, the sentence 'Give us this day our daily bread' is seen as unconvincing, because the word 'daily' is not needed in such a sentence as this; it duplicates itself, so it is almost unnecessary.

As noted earlier, the reason for the negative attitude to 'higher than substance' is that such a deep, transcendent-philosophical concept as a nutrient higher than physical substance is regarded as not possible for the Gospels; it is "alien to the (*philosophical-linguistic*) simplicity of the Gospels" (Lightfoot).[21]

So, eventually the version 'daily bread' gained prominence, and most Bibles use it; e.g., the NRSV,

---

Divine Names", para. xi. #6). But his view is erroneous, as epi is used in this same way.
[21] In p.228

ESV, NIV, KJ, Luther (täglich Brot), and the NEB. Rudolf Steiner used the Luther version, in his lectures on the Prayer. I attribute this to his decision to use the well-known and revered Luther text, as he had not presented an esoteric translation, to any audience.

However, before contemplating nutrition spiritually with the help of Rudolf Steiner's work, there is another important clue as to the nature of 'the bread' that is meant in the prayer. This further understanding also comes from Jerome.

The lost "Gospel according to the Hebrews"
A Hebrew version of the Lord's Prayer was included in the so-called *Gospel of the Hebrews*. It was known to the great fourth century scholar, Jerome, whose translation of the Greek and Hebrew Scriptures led to the Vulgate Bible. He possessed a copy of this lost Gospel. However, this is not the lost, original Hebrew version of the *Gospel of Matthew* – that is a different text. The *Gospel according to the Hebrews* today has survived only in fragments. It was probably written early in the second century, in Palestine.

The actual nature of this Gospel remains unclear, as only a few passages from it have survived. It was consulted by early church Fathers, but today scholars disagree about just how important it was to the early church. Origenes and Eusebius,[22] who inherited the library of Origenes, both regarded it as a valuable text, using it in their commentary on the Gospels. Origenes, although signalling that it is not a universally accepted text, quotes a passage from this lost Gospel, where it recounts that the mother of Jesus was the Holy Spirit;

---

[22] His dates are approx. AD 260 to 339.

"If anyone wishes to accept the *Gospel to the Hebrews*, where the Saviour himself says, 'My mother, the Holy Spirit, took me by one of my hairs and carried me off to the great mountain Tabor', that person shall question how the 'mother' of Christ is able to be the Holy Spirit, who was created by the Word."[23]

The topic of what the mother of Jesus was, in esoteric, cosmic terms, is not our concern here; it is to show that Origenes regarded this now lost Gospel as having some authority.

Furthermore, Jerome quoted or referred specifically to, this lost Gospel several times, and Clement of Alexandria also quoted from it. However Jerome, when commenting on the Lord's Prayer in this unusual Hebrew Gospel only quotes one word from it. Yet, other Hebrew texts of the Lord's Prayer have survived; in manuscripts from the Middle Ages.

It is significant that, in these medieval Hebrew documents, which have their origin in the early years of Christianity, the same word is used as that which Jerome preserved (see below).

What does 'Mahar' mean?
From an examination of Jerome's Latin text, I conclude that Jerome has made an error of judgement in his interpretation of this word. For in his *Commentary on Matthew's Gospel*, he records that, in this now lost *Gospel to the Hebrews*, the

---

[23] Origenes' comment on the Gospel, Ἐὰν δὲ προσιῆταί τις τὸ καθ' Εβραιους εὐανγγέλιον, ἔνθα αὐτὸς ὁ σωτήρ φησιν .... in ΟΙΓΕΝΟΥΣ, ΤΩΝ ΕΙΣ ΤΟ ΚΑΤΑ ΙΩΑΝΝΗΝ ΕΥΑΓΓΕΛΙΟΝ ΕΞΗΓΤΙΚΩΝ (Origenes, *Commentary on the Gospel of John* vol. 1) Cecile Blanc, edit. Editions Du Cerf, Paris, p. 264, 1996.

Hebrew word there is "רהמ". That is, Jerome writes out these three Hebrew letters. He then comments:

"this word means: tomorrow's. So the sense is, 'give us today tomorrow's, that is, *future* bread."

We discuss what these letters may mean, below. Now, one reason that Jerome made this conclusion is probably that 'epiousion', as explained above, can be interpreted to mean 'for tomorrow' or 'for the coming day'. So the two words, Greek and Hebrew, then seem to support each other as each apparently means 'tomorrow's. However, I hope to show that this is not the case.

I have not found any scholarly work which has carefully assessed Jerome's conclusions about the Hebrew word, so I have attempted to do this. I shall endeavour to show that Jerome's conclusion regarding this Hebrew word is invalid. Firstly, the various reports of Jerome's text in scholarly books, stating that Jerome said 'mahar', are themselves not valid.

For Jerome literally wrote (translating now his text from Latin),

"...instead of supersubstantialis bread, I found רהמ which means *tomorrow's*."

That is, Jerome in writing out these three consonants did not write out an actual Hebrew word.[24]

Now it is precisely here that it appears to me that Jerome has made an error, although apparently

---

[24] This is his actual Latin text, "....pro supersubstantialis pane, reperit רהמ, quod dicitur *crastinum* .."Jerome, *Commentariorum In Evangelium Matthei, Libri Quattuor* (*Commentary on Matthew*) 1.6.11; p.44.

this has not been noticed over the centuries. The above three Hebrew letters don't necessarily spell 'tomorrow'. In fact, these three letters do not spell any word at all. For in the ancient Hebrew literary tradition, only the consonants were written down, the vowels were left out.

So only these three consonants, (which in English are 'MHR') were written in the Gospel to the Hebrews; there were no vowels. Vowels were added only in the 6th century after Christ. So what other word might these three letters form, depending on which vowels are added?

In the modern world, the Hebrew lexicon universally used by Christian scholars is that one developed by the Rev. W. Gesenius, a 19th century German Christian theologian. It is regarded as a comprehensive lexicon (dictionary) of ancient Hebrew for scholars of the Old Testament.

Because this 930-page book was written in back in the 1820's, three British scholars in 1906 updated this book, since knowledge of Semitic linguistics had been substantially refined since the 1820's; it was enlarged to 1,156 pages.

However, there was a substantially better Hebrew lexicon, which is no longer available. A brilliant Jewish student of Rev. Gesenius, namely Julius Fürst, wrote the finest Hebrew lexicon. Fürst became a very learned scholar of Hebrew, Aramaic, Syriac, Arabic and Coptic.

As a Jew, Fürst immersed himself in Hebrew and Aramaic literature to a degree far exceeding that of Gesenius; in fact he wrote a three-volume bibliography of all known Hebrew and Aramaic texts from antiquity to the 19th century.

In the 1860's Fürst wrote the largest, most comprehensive Lexicon of biblical Hebrew, totaling some 1,400 pages; but this comprehensive Hebrew lexicon has long been unavailable.[25]

The immense scholarship of Fürst offers an important contribution to solving this enigma: namely that the three consonants written down by Jerome can result in six words, depending on what the writer meant; that is, which vowels are added mentally by the reader, and also which syllables are accented.

An edition of this lexicon from 1863 is in my library and from a study of this lexicon (and other smaller reference works) it becomes clear that the three consonants MHR can form 6 different words, which together have about nine meanings.

I should note here that the Lord's Prayer was no doubt spoken to the disciples in Aramaic by Jesus. But from the comments of Jerome, and research by various scholars, I have concluded that sometimes the Gospel was written down by some Christians in Hebrew, by others in Aramaic.

My conclusion here is helpful in addressing the complex topic, discussed in great detail by various scholars, as to whether the Gospel of Matthew was originally written in Hebrew or Aramaic.[26]

---

[25] I am not referencing the 8 vol. Dictionary of Classical Hebrew (edit. D. Clines), although it is huge, it does not include any significant additional material regarding OT texts, but other Hebrew texts.

[26] This question is very complex, and is further complicated by the fact that the Gospels include some Aramaic terms, together with quotes from the Hebrew Scriptures (translated into Greek). For example, Prof. Luz concluded that the reference to 'debts' in the Prayer has to be from an Aramaic word which means both financial as well as moral indebtedness, as 'no equivalent word exists in Hebrew'. But the Heb. 'ashahm' (אָשָׁם) in my view does cover these two aspects, as in Gen. 26:10 and

What these three letters can mean:
1: to flow on/ run on/ be in motion

2: morning, tomorrow, or a futural event

3: hastily, quickly.

4: to exchange, or to offer up (to something)

5: to offer up (to something)/ and also: to immerse/ let pour into/ exchange for/ let flow into

6: a dowry (this noun can be a verb, meaning 'to offer up something of value'.

So the Fürst dictionary reports five more meanings to the letters MHR, as different vowels are added to create words, than the standard BDB lexicon based on Gesenius' work. These are namely: to run on, move on, let flow into, immerse, as well as – very significantly – to offer (oneself) up; and indeed in two words.[27]

So there were six possible words – which together have about 9 meanings – from which Jerome could decide; not just 'tomorrow'. And very significantly, two of the words mean 'to offer up', suggestive of a sacrificial offering. One of these words gave rise to another word for something that metamorphoses or transforms itself.

In the Hebrew Scriptures (or Old Testament) there are 40 usages of these three letters; 38 of which can result in the word for 'haste'. One results in 'the future', whilst the other results in 'giving over' or a sacrificial surrendering of something. Jerome decided on the 'futural' meaning, since 'haste' was not relevant; he apparently dismissed the other possible words, or was unaware of them.

Levit. 5:15, 14:12, where sin requires a financial payment (although in livestock or grains, etc).
[27] ‚offer up': in Fürst's German: 'hingeben'.

35

It is my conclusion that the meaning of 'offering up', or 'sacrificing something to another', is what Matthew meant in his original Hebrew Gospel. Before contemplating this Hebrew word further, let's see the confusion that prevailed around this word, whether in the Hebrew or the Greek.

A Survey of the Interpretations in the Early Church

For this, I am indebted to the very learned research of the 19th century scholar Bishop Lightfoot, who wrote the most comprehensive study of how this word was used, although his study was limited by the prevailing humanistic orientation.

Here are the various translations, from either Hebrew or Greek, of the word about the petition for bread:

1st to 3rd century Latin: "daily"
Later Latin: "above (earthly) substance"
Later Greek: "necessary for the body's substance"
Syriac, early 4th cent: "continual"
Syriac, later 4th cent: "of necessity"
Coptic, 3rd century: "of tomorrow"
lost Gospel to the Hebrews: MHR (as noted above)
Medieval Hebrew: (see below)

One sees from this confusion, that the meaning is not obvious; a broader spiritual perspective helps the researcher to understand what is meant.

Another Hebrew indicator about 'the bread'.

We have discovered that in the lost *Gospel to the Hebrews*, the word 'mahar' was used, which can mean a sacrificially giving up something to another; but there is another Hebrew witness. For theologians are aware that in the 14th century, Jewish scholars had a Hebrew version of the

Gospel of Matthew. This medieval text had its origins in an unknown earlier century, and had been used for centuries by Jewish scholars to criticize its contents.

The question that is discussed by New Testament scholars is, whether this Hebrew text, in parts, is an accurate copy of an original Gospel of Matthew written in Hebrew. It is generally accepted by scholars, from statements made by early church authorities,[28] that Matthew did write out his Gospel in Aramaic (as well as Greek), but that text has been lost. It is also likely that a Hebrew version was made as well.

Some theologians have decided that this medieval Hebrew version of the Gospel of Matthew does generally retain an accurate record of the original Hebrew version of Matthew's Gospel, despite some centuries of editorial activity, although some experts are not sure.

I conclude that a medieval version of the Gospel in Hebrew, as used by Jewish scholars, does preserve much of the first century Gospel in Hebrew. What is interesting here is that the medieval versions, used by Jewish scholars have this sentence for the fourth petition:
"Give us our continual bread"

We have seen above, that the early Syrian text also has 'continual'. Why do these Hebrew-derived Syriac versions have 'continual' ? The Hebrew text for 'continual' is 'tamid' (תָּמִיד) which is a normal ancient Hebrew word; its grammatical meaning is quite clear.

---

[28] Comments to this effect were made by Papias, Origenes, Eusebius and Epiphanius.

But why was it used? I conclude that those who acquired the Syriac version, perhaps as early as the first century, concluded wrongly that the letters MHR meant 'mahar', meaning 'tomorrow's bread', just as Jerome had also erroneously concluded on one occasion. So they read the Hebrew sentence as, "Give us daily our bread for tomorrow".

I conclude that then those who had acquired the Hebrew version of the Gospel, later abbreviated the original sentence in their copies, thinking that, if each day we are helped to receive bread for tomorrow, then this bread (i.e., nutrition) is ongoing or continual; there is no interruption in supply of this food. Therefore, they wrote out a shorter version of the sentence,
        "Give us our continual bread".

So both the copy of Matthew's Gospel acquired by some hostile Hebrew scholars, and lost *Gospel to the Hebrews*, had 'MHR' as a description of the 'bread'. This is a reliable indicator that Matthew's original Hebrew Gospel did indeed have the letters MHR to describe the bread. However, by this word, Matthew did not mean 'tomorrow's bread', but rather, "...bread that (sacrificially) gives itself over to us (for our body)."

That is, these same letters (MHR) which were in the lost *Gospel to the Hebrews*, to which Jerome had access, is also in the text acquired by, and copied by, sceptical Hebrew scholars, (but which was later shortened).

As G. Howard has very capably argued, it is not the case that these Hebrew scholars obtained the Greek version of the Gospel of Matthew, and then translated this entire Greek text into Hebrew, and in doing this translated 'epiousion' into MIIR, meaning 'tomorrow's bread'.[29]

I agree with Howard and H. Schonfield that the Hebrew version of Matthew's Gospel, as acquired by Jewish scholars, was not created by translating a Greek text of Matthew's Gospel back into Hebrew, but it is a copy of an ancient version of the Hebrew-language Gospel. Schonfield makes reference to statements from Epiphanius in the fourth century that a Hebrew version of the Gospel of Matthew was kept in Jewish archives in Tiberias.[30]

So, the earliest Greek versions have 'epiousion' which means bread that is of nobler/finer substance (than our body's substances). Whilst the ancient Hebrew word MHR indicates a nourishment which sacrifices itself, with perhaps the further implication of it thereby becoming transformed.

So it appears that 'epiousion' is not a translation into Greek of 'mahar'; it conveys a different meaning to the Hebrew word, but a meaning which is compatible with it.

Why these different meanings in the early Hebrew version as compared to the early Greek version? When someone wrote out the long-lost *Gospel to the Hebrews* we may conclude they took the words of the Lord's Prayer directly from the Hebrew version of the Gospel of Matthew.

The word which the Jewish reader would have understood to be meant was 'mahar', meaning something which is 'given-over' or sacrificially

---

[29] G. Howard, *The Hebrew Gospel of Matthew*, Mercer University Press, 1995.
[30] In Epiphanius *Against Heresies* 30:3,6. Noted by Schonfield in his *An Old Hebrew Text of St. Matthew's Gospel,* T & T Clark, Edinburgh, 1917.

made available to, another person or entity. So the Hebrew text of the Lord's Prayer was indicating that this 'bread' is a subtle nutrient, which selflessly yields itself up to the person, to become part of their bodily substance.

Whereas when the Hebrew Gospel was translated into Greek, probably by Matthew himself or those close to him, a special word was coined (epiousion) which has a different meaning. It points to a nutrient beyond, or finer than, physical substance; a subtle nourishment which 'God' enables humanity to absorb.

These two descriptions, though different, are mutually supportive; together they mean that we are hoping to absorb subtle nutrient for the physical body which is superior to our usual physical substance, and which willingly sacrifices itself, transforms itself, by being absorbed into our body.

On the basis of these points, the esoteric meaning of this first petition in the Lord's Prayer is unveiled. The nourishment that is prayed for here is a subtle ethereal energy that in effect sacrifices itself in giving itself over to be absorbed into the human body.

There is also the possible implication that in doing this, the ethereal energy ('non-substance') is itself transformed, or metamorphosed. This plea is not about asking that we have enough food to eat each day. As Rudolf Steiner commented,
"...this verse in the Lord's Prayer has a greater meaning than a (mundane, pragmatic) plea that we may daily receive food – more than we can get through our own efforts."[31]

---

[31] In book no. 92, p. 475.

We can note here that animals and plants are in a sense sacrificing themselves, when people consume them. Animals do so unwillingly, whilst edible plants it seems – that is, the spirits that have created these – do so willingly.

But it seems that the ethereal 'elemental' energy from which the plants are condensed into material substance, is neutral in this process. If people have a 'grace before meals', directing thereby their attention to this finer, non-material matrix of the plants, this inner effort results in the ethereal energies becoming absorbed.

According to Rudolf Steiner, it is our life-forces or the 'etheric body' which is a primary agent in the process of digestion.[32] He taught that it is this 'etheric body' which has the task of transforming the food particles that enter the stomach, and then revitalizing these particles and preparing them for absorption, especially the finer, etherealized components of the food, which arises as a result of this absorption process.[33] See below for more about this theme of ethereal energies behind our food.

Plea 4 - now combining the Hebrew and the Greek terms
correlates to our life-forces (etheric body)

Give to us daily our bread; the 'bread' which is higher than physical substance, which offers itself up to us.

Contemplating the further meaning of the fourth plea

---

[32] For example in book 107 in the Complete Works, (p. 69.)
[33] Book no. 128, p. 154, and book no. 218, lect. of 22nd Oct. 1922.

Behind the physical substance of our food, there is a subtle life-force maintaining the molecular substance of our foods. This life-force can be absorbed, making the person's physical-flesh body less dense, less coarse.

Rudolf Steiner referred to the body's flesh as being either 'denser' or less dense – in a subtle way, not necessarily detectable to scientific instruments. He comments that the physical body was less dense in remote times. But in today's world this quality will vary, depending on various factors, including one's diet and also mental-emotional 'diet'. This petition in the Lord's Prayer is pointing to a nutritional factor that determines how subtly hardened or sensitive is the body. In this prayer, one is requesting that, when eating, the ethereal energies may be absorbed by us from our food.

Rudolf Steiner taught that our higher consciousness – that is, the capacity to be an intuitive thinker, a spiritually insightful person – depends upon the body being less 'dense', that is, not being coarsened or 'hardened'. We can more easily grasp what he is saying, if we consider a person who were to eat primarily denatured, over-processed, stodgy foods with a high proportion of fatty flesh; their consciousness could become somehow 'heavy' and inert.

So this petition is asking that the Divine assist us each day, with regard to the physical body, by enabling us to receive and absorb the finer, ethereal elements present within our nutrition.

The purpose of this petition is for our soul-spirit to obtain a 'harvest' for its own further spiritualization from a consciously intuitive engagement with life's experiences; by not having this opportunity lost through the effect of a sluggish body upon our consciousness; a body whose density muffles the more subtle spiritual insights.

The nourishment higher than our physical body
This concept, that there is an invisible ethereal energy behind plant and animal substances, was a well-established truth in the Hellenistic Age, including amongst Jewish scholars. The writings of Philo Judaeus are very relevant here. He was a contemporary of Jesus, but lived in Alexandria, Egypt. He taught an esoteric wisdom developed from Hellenistic Judaism. When writing about the creation of the world, he gives a key perspective on the nature of our foodstuffs, which points to the meaning of this word, epiousion;

"For as our Creator divided our souls and our limbs in the middle, he also likewise divided the non-physical substance of the cosmos, when he made the Earth."

Philo goes on to explain that God subdivided the non-physical 'substance' (that is, life-energies and soul energies) of our planet into heavy and buoyant types; and these were again divided into denser or more subtle parts;
"Then from these, God condensed air and fire, and also water and earth. Then God formed the four 'elements' as sense-perceptible or physical elements (condensed from the finer invisible 'elements')."

A passage in the initiatory *Hermetica* text commenting on this same topic, states, "From these four elements our bodies receive nutriment which comes from them, and this nutriment renews our bodies each day…this process holds the body together."[34]

---

[34] Excerpt 5, "Hermes to Tat'.

Philo later comments that the four physically perceptible elements "were designed to serve as the foundations of the sense-perceptible world." He then writes a comment of huge significance to our attempt to understand the word 'epiousion'; "from these four 'elements' which were separated off from the invisible, non-physical universal 'substance', the plants and animals were condensed (or coagulated) ...then by means of these (four elements), animals and plants were condensed (out of the ether)".[35]

It is crucial here to realize, that these four states of matter or four 'elements' have coagulated out of the all-encompassing ethereal 'elements'. So too, our foodstuffs – like the four states of matter – are condensed out of the invisible ethereal energies which envelop our planet. It was known in the Hellenistic Age that the supposedly empty air was permeated by an all-enveloping ethereal 'aura'. In the Hermetica this is succinctly stated, "All of the firmament is pervaded by air and the Ether."[36]

So what is the 'bread' higher than physical substance" ?

It is the ethereal energies from which the physical foodstuff was condensed (or coagulated) into physical substance via the four elements. There is an old German prayer or 'grace before meals', which points to this same reality:

> "The bread from the grain,
> the grain from the light,
> the light from God's countenance divine;
> May the light live on
> in this heart of mine."

---

[35] His Grk. in *Quis Rerum Divinarum Heres*, 27: καὶ τὰ διὰ τούτων παγέντα ζωα(ι) τε καὶ φυτα(ι).
[36] In the Grk. *Kore Kosmou* Exc. 23, Ἔστω πεπληρωμένος ὁ οὐρανὸς ἅπασιν ἀήρ τε καὶ αἰθήρ

Rudolf Steiner emphasizes that the process of digestion is a process involving our soul. In particular it is the subconscious will which is the veiled power that is responsible for breaking down and then absorbing, the tiny, altered particles extracted from the food (via one's etheric body). These are the two dynamics that underlie the process of replenishing the substances of our body.

We can note here that to the sensitive observer, there is a definite consciousness active within our immune system, and in our digestion processes. In the anthroposophical view this consciousness **is us**: it is our will, which is primarily subconscious. Before assessing Steiner's words, it is helpful to consider that our food is digested in three stages:

Consciously: in the mouth - its digestive fluids can turn a carbohydrate into sugar, and we can be very aware of that.

Semi-consciously: in the stomach - its acidic fluids break down proteins; and we can be vaguely aware of that, especially if the digestive process is not successful, for then uncomfortable sensations are the result.

Subconsciously
In the duodenum and the small intestines together: digesting vitamins, fats and minerals, and generally breaking down nutrients received from the stomach into even smaller particles. We can have no consciousness of the digestive processes occurring in these organs; and yet these processes do occur, in all their astonishing complexity.

(There are other aspects of our subconscious soul energies to which we do not have access; and yet, through effort, we can improve our health, by endeavouring to become attuned to, and support, some of the tasks regulated by our immune system.)

So this fourth petition is not about a deity directly giving us a higher ethereal nutrient, but about the person when digesting food, asking for help from the Divine, for us to be more sensitive to, and thus more empowered in our consciousness, regarding the capacity to absorb finer ethereal nutrients in the food.

This help is invoked by one's own inner efforts to make one's veiled soul powers especially empowered – and the implication of the prayer is that divine beings in spirit worlds (or 'God') assist this process in us.

It appears to me that the above conclusions about the deeper meaning of this fourth plea are compatible with a brief indicator from Rudolf Steiner. In his few lectures on the theme of 'our 'bread' he did not unveil this deeper meaning. But in one lecture he hinted at this by saying enigmatically,
"The physical body can only develop itself in a healthy manner if we permit the 'daily bread' to approach it **in the right way**."[37]
(emphasis mine, AA)
So these words point to a consciously undertaken process, through which the person becomes actively involved in the consuming of food. The aim of this is to enhance the absorption of the subtle life-force behind the physical substance.

In summary: the meaning of epiousion from initiatory wisdom
When the Gospel of Matthew was written out in Greek, the word 'epiousion' was especially created to direct our attention to the idea that a subtle

---

[37] In book no. 100, p. 73 (lect. of 21st June 1907).

nutrient for our body is available, and this is superior to our own bodily substance.

Now, to fully unveil the esoteric meaning of this unique word, we note that 'ousias' also means 'one's **own** possessions'; for example, one's own property. But since this petition to the Divine, or God, is about the physical body, it means the physical substance of one's own body, because this, the first of the four lower petitions, is about our physical body; so it needs to be contemplated in that context.

We also note here that the noun 'ousias' (substance) is closely related to the ancient Greek verb 'ousio-oe' (ὀυσιόω) meaning, 'to imbue someone with being, or with substance'.)

So the Greek text of the prayer is requesting that nutrient may be absorbed which is superior to, or finer than, the matter in our own physical-material body. So 'our epiousion bread' actually means: a nutrient which shall soon be part of us, by **imbuing our body with something higher, more subtle** than what we may get by simply swallowing our physical food. The prayer is asking that we be helped by directing our mind to assimilating the finer, ethereal energies permeating physical food.

But why does this matter? Why would the cosmic Christ include a petition about the body? The reason is, as noted above, our consciousness, in regard to comprehending spiritual truths, or intuiting spiritual reality, is directly affected, depending on whether the body's substance is subtly hardened and coarse, or lighter, and more refined.

The life-force above material substance.
We have seen above that in the Hellenistic Age, the four elements underpinning physical existence

were understood to have condensed out of four other, ethereal, non-physical levels of these elements. All plant and flesh foodstuffs are permeated by a life-force – and so when we eat food, the accompanying life-force of the foodstuff is absorbed as well.

This core fact is of course excluded from materialistic science; but one only has to consider what would happen if someone were to have a diet in which all the components of their food – vitamins, oils, minerals, carbohydrates, proteins – were to be artificially made. That is, manufactured from minerals (i.e., chemicals) and not absorbed from plants or animals, as created by nature out of the ethers.

Such a person would soon become seriously ill. Science is unaware of the subtle yet vital role that the life-forces of nature has in our nutritional needs; just as it is unaware of the crucial role that the life-force entity (or 'etheric-body') has in our cognitional capacity. (And in the life of our planet.)

An astounding example of this blindness is, as Rudolf Steiner points out, that science is fully correct in observing how, when we see or hear a sense object, this sensory experience becomes only a chemical reaction in the eye or ears, as well as electrical nerve signals.

This fact should mean that all of our sensory experiences are illusions, since scientific research cannot detect in the brain any tiny image of an object we are looking, or a musical note we hear. But in fact we do indeed see and hear sensory sights and sounds; this presents an unsolvable riddle to science.

The answer to this enigma is that every sensory perception not only impacts the physical body, but is also absorbed by the life-forces behind the body's sense organs. It is this energy-body which receives and stores the image of a flower or the sound of a musical note, etc.

So, the fourth plea is a prayer that we may be sensitive to, or mindful of, the possibility for our body to absorb the life-forces that permeate our food. It was from these ethereal energies that our foodstuffs were condensed into their physical state. Being aware of this capacity enhances our ability to absorb those ethereal energies and the more this happens, the finer, the less dense the body becomes.

In this process the life-forces are given over to the human's physical-etheric body; this is a somewhat sacrificial process, similar to that by which plants or animals surrender themselves over to the human being, to be consumed.

Of these two dynamics, one is mirrored in the Greek term epiousion; and the other by the Hebrew word 'mahar'.

Hence the fourth plea is:
Give to us daily our bread; the 'bread' which is higher than physical substance (of our own body), which offers itself up to us.

We now move to a consideration of the fifth plea:
FIFTH PLEA:
correlates to: our life-forces or etheric body

**"and forgive us our moral debts
as we forgive those who have become
indebted to us,"**

(The traditional version:
"And forgive us our debts as we have forgiven our debtors..."

As with every plea of this immensely deep cosmic prayer, this fifth plea has a deeper meaning which is discernible to an initiatory perspective. So traditional translations, like that given above, cannot convey its deeper meaning, especially if the correct word 'debts' is replaced with 'sins' or 'trespasses' (see below).

Before considering this plea, it is helpful to firstly consider the very idea of one's sins being somehow no longer a threat; i.e., of being 'forgiven'. All religions across the globe from ancient times have several social-spiritual reasons for their existence. One is that the priesthoods of antiquity possessed some clairvoyance or 'higher' awareness, and thus the intentions of various deities inhabiting their part of the earth, and other deities perceptible to their spiritual vision, were very important to them. The priesthoods felt the necessity of being informed about what these deities required of their people.

But another major reason for the existence of religions, is that the general community felt the need to be protected by their central deity from harm; harm that may be imminent, and caused by the 'sins' that they had committed. The harm could occur in daily life, as in apparently natural events that damaged their crops and livestock, or in the existence after death, where wrathful deities awaited them.

This conviction that 'God' (in the case of the Hebrews, this is Jahve) gives protection from the consequences of sins, was central to the religion of the ancient Hebrews, and is specifically affirmed in a several passages; "I, even I, am He that blots out your transgressions for my own sake, and will not remember your sins." (Isa.43:25), and "To the Lord our God belongs mercies and forgivenesses, for we have rebelled against Him." (Dan. 9:9)

In the modern era, amidst the so pervasive materialism, and consequent decline of religion, this conviction has greatly faded. The Lord's Prayer was, of course, given in a time when these concerns were still acutely felt. But actually the reference to forgiveness in the Prayer points to a different context; it teaches us that for the human being to be free of potential punishment for an ongoing inherent lack of 'godliness', each person must learn to forgive anyone who has, some time ago, done something wrong to them; or who is persisting with a malignant attitude regarding them.

The pointer to the actual esoteric meaning is the word 'debt'. This is a striking term; one would expect here the word 'sin', in fact, some old manuscripts have been altered by scribes to have the word 'sin'.

The reason for this unusual term 'debt' is revealed through initiatory insight; it points to an on-going, persistent interaction between oneself and other persons.

This word 'debt' means in normal financial terms that someone is obligated to another person, and this obligation, which has the power of a contractual arrangement, has been incurred some time ago; so it is ongoing, but will have to be dealt with in the future. Hence this fifth plea is about the on-going negative influences darkening the 'ether' around us from someone's on-going, persistent ill-will.

Rudolf Steiner explains that with this fifth plea, the human 'etheric-body' is involved; which is that member of the sevenfold human being that is a stage above the physical body. Our 'etheric body' is in effect our life-forces, and these energies determine our predisposition or temperament.

Our soul may specifically and sporadically manifest unethical desires, thoughts or intentions. These can flare up, coming and going, lasting minutes or hours. Whereas the situation with our life-forces or 'etheric body' is quite different.

If a nasty deed is carried out against us, its damaging effects can linger on in us and in our social group for years. Also if we allow a negative reaction in our own soul to this deed to intensify, then this persistent soul-mood reaches down into the life-forces (or etheric body) and there it takes root, becoming a persistent semi-conscious tendency or what we call our predisposition.

But on the other hand, someone who opposes us can maintain a dislike of us for months or years, with only a very slight reason, or indeed from no valid reason at all. This on-going attitude can then become an habitual tendency within their life-energies (or etheric body); and we can reciprocate, developing an animosity towards them.

Such 'sinful' ways of being, persisting on for a long period of time, are the moral equivalent of a financial debt. They can exist for a considerable time, but at some point in the future they will have to be 'paid off'; they cannot be simply ignored. Just as a debt is a burden in everyday life, this habitual antagonism poisons the ethers; that is, the subtle life-energies in the world around us.

Having habitual sinfulness 'neutralized'
Long-term feelings and thoughts in our soul have an effect on our life-forces. This in turn forms part of our predisposition or 'temperament', and hence may include any persistent grudge or dislike of another person; this may be semi-conscious. But this creates a kind of indebtedness to that disliked person, because we are thereby raying out from

our aura some disturbing, even harmful energies that darken that person's path through life.

So if someone else is doing that to us, they become in effect spiritually indebted to us; they will have to make good the difficulties their attitude has caused us, and which has burdened the 'energy' of our community (i.e., its life-forces).

This verse in the Lord's Prayer is urging us to be aware of the moral imperative to extinguish any grudging, simmering, antipathy towards that person. This requires the offending person to become responsive to their conscience; to do this is to extinguish these on-going attitudes. This removes the toxic energies between us and them; and thereby helps to bring harmony into the 'ether' of the world around us.

As Rudolf Steiner taught, the plea is about "the balancing-out of that which has occurred through the imperfections in the etheric body".[38] So in effect, this plea and the duties it places upon us, have the goal for us, of 'attaining harmony with the social reality of our community'.[39]

So by using the word 'debt', the Lord's Prayer is pointing us towards this simmering persistent unwholesome influence in the life-energies around us, and also between us and our fellow human beings. The concern of this plea is not about a 'sin' as such. For the issues around being 'sinful' that is, unethical, are fairly clear; but the sage or clairvoyant is acutely aware of the specific burden laming the Earth's life-forces from habitual negative attitudes. People who are spiritually sensitive can also intuit this.

---

[38] In book no. 96, p. 218.
[39] In book no. 100, lect. 21st June 1907.

So from this deeper perspective, it appears to me helpful to add in brackets, some extra words to this plea (as above). But these revelations now call upon us to more deeply understand the idea of a moral debt being 'forgiven'. What does it mean to 'forgive' someone? We need to firstly examine whether the plea is 'we forgive' or 'we have forgiven'.

Forgive or forgiven ?
The usual decision of translators for this plea is to use the past tense "for we have forgiven...."; but I have used "for we forgive...". The situation here is that scholars cannot state which of these two grammatical possibilities is correct. For two highly regarded codices, Sinaiticus and Vaticanus, as well as a 6th century text in Dublin, and about 10 other older texts have 'we have forgiven...'

Whereas the very important codex Bezae and virtually all of the many other ancient versions of the Gospel still in existence, in Greek, Coptic, Armenian and Ethiopian, etc, have 'for we forgive', or 'we are forgiving': that is, in the present tense.

I have decided upon 'we forgive' for two reasons. One is that this present-tense version is also found in several medieval Hebrew versions of the Gospel of Matthew. In particular, in the impressive 'Shem-tob' manuscript, which Howard argues does preserve the original Hebrew version of the Gospel, which was written in the first century.

The second reason is that the present tense makes it clear that this 'forgiving' is a continuous process, as new hostilities can arise. Moreover, a renewal of our 'forgiving' regarding an earlier incident can be needed.

Forgiving or being released from: an initiatory perspective revealing a new aspect to the release from 'sins'

The Initiatory Quest pathway to assessing the Gospels enables us to understand more deeply this potent theme of sins being forgiven. It is through esoteric Christianity that one becomes aware that there are two aspects to how 'God' or the spiritual worlds may respond to a human sinful deed, or to an over-all sinfulness.

Deity can 'forgive' our general inherent sinfulness, that is, our un-spiritual or 'un-godly' habitual ways of being, as earthly people. This means that corrective punishment for such qualities or ways of being is not decreed, whether in our existence after death, or, once we factor in repeated earth lives, karmically (meaning in a future incarnation).

If a deity 'forgives' a human being for 'un-godly' habitual ways of being, then corrective punishment is not required by the dynamics which underpin the cosmos.

But now in referring to the concept of repeated earth-lives, I need to refer to a discovery of mine, which, I realize is deeply challenging for devout mainstream Christians. For it has been understood throughout 2,000 years, that once a person becomes deliberately and sincerely a Christian, then the Saviour has forgiven that person for their 'sins', and hence eternal salvation in a heavenly realm is assured, when this one life is over.

This deeply comforting view of life is quite different to the perspective that arises when the esoteric or wider view of our existence is considered. Then the conclusion is that, the Saviour can and indeed does forgive our general 'un-godliness' and minor unethical deeds and traits.

But bearing in mind the words of Jesus that "Sins against the Holy Spirit will not be forgiven" one concludes that all qualities and deeds that are directly hostile to the Divine, to God, are significantly unethical, and then these are not 'forgiven'. They become part of one's karmic reality, and hence oppressive consequences will occur in the Hereafter, and in the next incarnation.

This reality is precisely what Christ seeks to help us with. Here discovery of the second kind of response to 'sins' by the Divine becomes important. My research into this profound theme established that, in the Gospels, when we are urged to forgive other people, whether in the Lord's Prayer or in other teachings of Jesus, the Greek word 'aphiaemi' (ἀφιημι) is used.

But, there are five occasions in the Gospels when in translation the 'forgiveness of sins' is the theme, but this translation is incorrect for these five places. For the Greek word used in these times is 'aphesis' (ἄφεσις), which does not mean to forgive. The word 'aphesis' is a noun formed from the other word, a verb, 'aphiaemi'. But whenever the noun is used in the NT, with regard to 'sin', it refers to the cancelling of, or release from, sins; not forgiving them. So the few references in the Greek-English lexicons of Thayer and Bauer, about 'aphesis' as meaning 'forgiving' are in my view erroneous.[40]

The usual word for forgiveness (aphiaemi) means: forgive, dissolve, or permit. But 'aphesis' is quite different, it means, the release or discharge from, or dismissal; and therefore in effect, 'cancel'.

---

[40] The paralysed man on the stretcher (Matt. 9:2) was told that, (from his suffering and renewed intentions towards a better morality, in the realm of the Dead, after his last life) his sins had *left* him, not 'forgiven' him; for 'aphiaemi' – which often means to forgive – here means to 'leave' or 'depart from'.

It appears that scholars are not aware that these two words have the above different meanings, (even though they are different forms of the same Greek word). They have this attitude because the spiritual reality behind karma is not included in their worldview. As a result, a truly sacred, core Gospel passage, from the event of the Last Supper, is translated as:

Matt. 26:28 'For this is my blood of the new covenant which is poured out for many, for the **forgiveness** of sins..."

But it should read, in my view:

Matt. 26:28: "For this is my blood of the new covenant which is poured out for many for **the release from** sinfulness."

For here, 'aphesis' is used; so 'release from' is meant here, not 'forgiveness of'. One could also say, "for the cancelling of sinfulness" because, as scholars are aware, the Greek word for sins (hamartia) also means 'sinfulness'.

There are five occasions in the Gospels where 'aphesis' is used[41] and translated as 'forgive', as noted earlier, but these can all mean 'to release', and I understand them to mean exactly that. There are also nine places where this happens in the Epistles,[42] and again in these places this the word means 'to release', and not 'to forgive'.

That is, Christ came to the Earth for the immensely more powerful purpose of giving release from sinfulness in the human soul, or one could also say, for cancelling sinfulness; this means in effect, to grant salvation. But this process normally requires

---

[41] These are: Mk. 1:4, 3:29 Lk. 1:77, 3.3, 4:18 and 24.47.
[42] These are: Acts 2:38, 5:31, 10:43, 13:38, 26:18 and Eph. 1:7, Col. 1:14, Heb. 9:22 and 10.18.

several lifetimes, rather than the less potent action of 'forgiving' a sin, although this is a valid help or blessing that Christ can give.

This is a very potent new perspective, because it brings in an extraordinary new, and for many people, challenging reality. The Divine can **cancel** that is, give us **release from** 'sinfulness'; this means that Christ seeks to bring the 'lower-self' or sinful nature of each person to an end, by helping the soul towards spirituality.

An ancient Christian text provides confirmation of my research, that a release from the lower-self is meant here, not forgiveness – and thereby a glorious blossoming of the higher 'Christ-self'. This text was written very early in the Christian world; either late in the first century or early in the second century.

It is known as *The Epistle of Barnabas*; its author is unknown. It is probably not written by the famous friend of St. Paul, but perhaps Barnabas taught or inspired the writer.

This epistle was cited by authoritative early church Fathers, including Flavius Clement of Alexandria, Origenes, Eusebius and Jerome. Jerome and Origenes regarded it as genuinely inspired. This Epistle was bound in the great Codex Sinaiticus, showing that it was widely regarded as an authoritative or inspired text in the fourth century.

In the extract we are considering here, the Epistle actually points out just how potent is the divine blessing which is conferred by the release from, (or cancelling of) sins, or sinfulness. The text in effect teaches that thereby Salvation comes to humanity, creating new redeemed, childlike human beings,

"He (Jesus) renewed us by releasing us from sinfulness. He thereby made us into people of a different type; so that we may experience[43] the soul becoming like that of children; indeed it is as if (*in so doing*) he is re-fashioning us." (6:13)[44]

What a wonderful insight this early Teacher had; for in contemplating these words, one realizes that his comments cannot refer to just the 'forgiving' of sins. For the Saviour seeks to cancel our sinfulness, or more literally, 'release' us from this.

This means that the soul-state of the human soul may be 'saved' from its 'fallen' state; but this Teacher adds that we may thereby ascend up to the exquisite spiritual purity that the little child has. This means having no yearning for sensuality, but instead the capacity for joy, from a feeling of awe and wonder and reverence – so one's soul is enveloped in, and sensitive to, the Good, the True and the Beautiful; just as little children are. In the words of Rudolf Steiner; "We need to re-awaken the spirituality of the little child in our adult personality – then is the Christ in us."[45]

As it was not appropriate in the first phase of the Christian religion for Christians to be taught the potent reality of us having repeated earth-lives, Christians have assumed for many centuries that this removal of the 'sinful nature' by Christ would happen for the sincere Christian in just one life. However, those on the Christian initiatory path are aware that this release from the sinful nature would normally require a number of lifetimes.

In my *Gospel of John*, I have presented substantial evidence that knowledge of repeated earth lives was known and accepted amongst the Pharisees

---

[43] Literally: "we may 'have' the soul becoming..."
[44] The Grk. is: επι οὖν ἀνακαινίσας ἡμᾶς ἐν τῇ ἀφέσει τῶν ἁμαρτιῶν, ἐποίησεν ἡμας ἄλλον τύπον, ὡς παιδίων ἔχειν τὴν ψυχήν, ὡς ἂν δὴ ἀναπλάσσοντος αὐτοῦ ἡμᾶς.
[45] In book no.127, lect. of 25/Feb/1911.

and also by close followers of Jesus. But Jesus did not wish to incorporate this concept into the wider circles of Christians.

This was because, as Rudolf Steiner explains, Christianity was to develop extensively in the world as the religion of the individual, that is, the strongly individuated person. This developmental phase requires isolation from a mystical, transcendent world-view, filled with other-worldly concerns and spiritual beings.

An ancient document from a third century Christian writer, Hippolytus of Rome, reports on the understanding of an esoteric Christian group about this theme. His report, *On the Refutation of all Heresies*, has preserved a brief reference to the theme of reincarnating from this group, and also, very significantly, their assertion that the Saviour did not want this theme to be publicly discussed,

"Then, because of the Saviour, **discussion ceases of reincarnation,** and so Faith is preached concerning the release from sins." (See Appendix 3)

This valuable report tells us that the theme of people being released from sinfulness, in the course of repeated life-times, was not to be discussed. As a result, the 'forgiveness of sins' was destined to become a (somewhat unclear) answer to the question of, how does God deal with our 'sinfulness'.

There are many passages in the Epistles of St. Paul wherein the forgiveness of sins, the salvation of our souls, is emphatically declared in definite terms, as a once-and-for-all process. Rather than attempting to dialogue in detail with the teachings of St. Paul, I will just confirm that the truth is, as Rudolf Steiner once commented, many Pauline statements are not in fact compatible with esoteric Christian wisdom.

As a Pharisee, Paul knew that the teachings of repeated earth lives formed a part of the inner teachings of Hellenistic Judaism, and in my view (and that of Rudolf Steiner) he would have accepted this concept as correct. But as we have noted earlier, this wider, potent concept was to be excluded from Christian theology.

So, the situation is that theology was to be formed within the limits imposed by a world-view in which repeated earth lives and hence karma, were to be excluded.

But the power of a nearly two-thousand year old conviction is intense; so people who wish to maintain the traditional view may refer to a verse in Psalm 103. This is one of various verses that have reinforced the view that we have but one life, and that God does forgive sins – that is, eradicates any threat to our happiness in the after-life,

"As far as the East is from the West, so far does he (JHVH) remove our transgressions from us."

I would point out that the deity referred to here is Jahve (also called Jehovah), and the lines are referring to the ancient Hebrew nation. Also, in the Hebrew Scriptures, any mention of the complex dynamics that reincarnation and karma create, is also avoided.

The concept in esoteric Christianity is quite different. Namely, that the cosmic Christ, as the leader of the 'Powers', and as a vessel of the sublime Logos in the Triune Godhead, has the task of helping all races and nations across the entire planet; and indeed from incarnation to incarnation.

Forgiving sin by humans
We humans cannot cancel out someone's sins, but we can 'forgive' sin, as the Lord's Prayer requires. What this means is, we can:

refrain from hatred of the other person
seek no revenge on that person
not allow an on-going, habitual grudge against that person

Moreover, as a completion of this 'forgiving', we can also:
pray that the 'sinner' finds their conscience
entrust any corrective punishment to the will of God (i.e., to the karma-guiding powers)

This is to treat them, if the 'sin' was not a heinous one, in a positive way (which is within one's will, a loving or kind way).

It is important to note here that we cannot, and should not, convince ourselves that a serious crime the person committed was not repulsive or horrific to us. We should not convince ourselves that our feelings are quite at peace about what happened. To be outraged, to be repelled, to be horrified beyond words, is entirely ethical.

This is not what 'to forgive' a person who has acted in an aggressive or even heinous manner against us requires of us. Rather, it requires that we do not reciprocate their hateful deed or inner state of being; in addition we may pray that they can eventually respond to their conscience. This is a form of love, in the sense of good-will towards that person. These words again:

"He (Jesus) renewed us by releasing us from sinfulness. He thereby made us into people of a different type; so that we may experience the soul like that of children, indeed it is as if (in so doing) he is re-fashioning us." (Barnab. 6:13)[46]

---

[46] The Grk. is: επι ούν ανακαινίσας ημάς εν τη αφέσει των αμαρτιών, εποίησεν ημας άλλον τύπον, ως παιδίων έχειν την ψυχήν, ως αν δη αναπλάσσοντος αυτού ημάς.

These are very significant words, for they declare that it is by the overcoming of the debased or 'fallen' earth-bound soul qualities, that the primal, 'unfallen' childlike spirituality can re-emerge; and that this is in effect, Salvation. Such a re-moulding process of the human soul can scarcely apply to a forgiving of a sin.

As Rudolf Steiner taught, the exquisite capacities of awe and wonder, of reverence and devotion, formed the inherent nature of the soul until the process of humanity incarnating into the material world commenced, millions of years ago. It is this holy quality that Jesus was, and which he brought with him; this is what makes the first Christmas night in Bethlehem so inspiring to our hearts today.

From this text, one can see that whoever wrote this ancient Epistle of Barnabas correctly understood 'aphesis' as meaning a cancelling of 'sinfulness', not a 'forgiving'.

From the research of Rudolf Steiner, one can conclude that it is this 'releasing from sinfulness' process which makes salvation possible. This process occurs because of the influences originating from the presence of the cosmic Christ within the Earth's aura, and by the specific intentions of the Saviour, Jesus, with regard to the individual human soul.

But to return now to the fifth plea of the Lord's Prayer, its focus is clearly not on a 'cancelling' of sins, but on the forgiveness of persistent negative influences. This is necessary to clear away malignant energies enveloping our existence.

So, the 5th plea again:

and forgive us our moral debts
   (incurred by our habitual spirit-
      estrangement)

as we forgive those who have become indebted to us,
   (through past sinful deeds or habitual
      ill-will)

Reviewing the fifth plea:
By our own underlying unethical ways, by our ongoing un-spiritual state of being, we incur a debt to 'God', that is to various divine beings, and to their spiritual realms. And God – that is, the dynamics that permeate Creation – work in the following way: that if we do allow an on-going, habitual hostility towards someone to exist in our soul, it will eventually enter into our life-energies (or etheric-body), and from there habitually radiate out an unwholesome influence in the ethers.

From the understanding that these dynamics arise when a negative state of mind is allowed to brood for some time, I have added the phrases specifying an 'habitual' way of being. Although 'habitual' is not in the Greek, it is directly implied by the unusual choice of the Greek word for 'debts', and not simply for 'sins'.

SIXTH PLEA: verse 6:13a.
correlates to: the soul (or soul-body)
A very widespread translation is:
   "Do not lead us into temptation".

If the fourth plea concerned the physical body, and the fifth concerned the life-forces, this sixth plea concerns the soul – its wishes, desires, thoughts and intentions. The dynamics of our being, of our soul or 'soul-body' also exist outside us in the Earth's aura, as a field of consciousness, composed of all the emotions, yearnings, thoughts, etc, of humanity.

But with this plea, we encounter an extremely baffling verse; namely a request to the Divine which is disturbing, or even unacceptable, to the majority of believers. For the above commonly found translation is not correct to the Greek. This is because the Greek word used here 'eispheroe' (εἰσφέρω) never means 'to lead', but 'to bring'.

Also, while word 'trial' is correct to the Greek word, it also means 'temptation'; and I conclude that temptation is what is meant. So when the ancient Greek is translated with 'bring' – which is the actual meaning of the verb, it reads:

13a: "**And may Thou not bring us into temptation...**"
kai mae eisenaekaes haemas eis peirasmon
 (καὶ μὴ εἰσενέγκῃς ἡμᾶς εἰς πειρασμόν)
The difference here is substantial, for 'to lead someone into trial' has the implication of a dynamic such as when a person takes a donkey by the reins and ensures that it goes where he or she leads it. Whereas 'bring us into temptation' is very different; here, the soul is subtly permeated, and stirred from without into having an unethical desire.

Without initiatory insight, this verse is extremely baffling, because it seems to imply that God can set out to cause people to enter into lower states of ethics – or at least into the strong possibility of failing ethically.

This confronting element is recognized by many theologians; and therefore many Bibles have the above translation with 'lead' and not 'bring'. In recent years the difficulty here has caused some churches to actually deny the Greek and translate the petition even more incorrectly. In December 2017 the French Catholic church changed the verse from "Do not submit us to temptation" to "Do not let us enter into temptation".

As noted above, the correct translation of the Greek verb is 'to bring' not 'to lead'; translations which use 'lead' are avoiding the implications of 'bring'. When this verse is approached through the esoteric Christian initiatory wisdom of Rudolf Steiner, it becomes acceptable, even if still very challenging.

The tension around the word 'bring' centres on the very deep theme of the relation of 'God' to evil. Just how it has become possible for evil to exist and torment humanity, is an immensely challenging and formidable theme. Hence very few scholars are at peace with the implication that God would bring a person's soul into immorality.

The erroneous selection of the word 'lead', which occurred as from the 19th century, has actually caused the Greek verb to be formally defined incorrectly in lexicons. These dictionaries were created during the late 19th century onwards, at the time when this erroneous translation was chosen, and this led to the dictionaries formally giving the wrong meaning to the Greek word.

This led to a misleading circular result, whereby students who consult these lexicons are led to believe that the Greek word does have this meaning, which in fact it does not.[47]

As regards the term, 'temptation', this is also often rejected in translations or Commentaries. The term 'trial' (or tribulation or testing-time) is used instead. These alternative terms are in fact quite

---

[47] Thus, Thayer's *Greek-English Lexicon* and W. Mounce's *Analytical Lexicon to the Grk. NT* both give 'to lead' as a meaning of this verb, but every Biblical text reference they cite actually means 'to bring'. Bauer's *Grk.-Engl. Lexicon*, is more perceptive, citing 'to lead' only as a *possible* alternative meaning to 'bring' for the same references as the above lexicons erroneously cite.

correct to the Greek, because the Greek word here does also have these other meanings.

Hence many theologians have opted for a translation which refers to 'trial', not 'temptation', because it is so challenging to refer to God bringing a person into temptation, whereas it is acceptable to talk about God 'leading' (not 'bringing') someone into a trial.

But I conclude that the verse is in fact about the soul being brought into temptation; this is because this verse is a plea with respect to our soul in its interrelationship with the spiritual influences present in our cosmos. So the process which Christ means here, is one in which there is **a possible bringing us into temptation**, not a leading us into a carefully pre-determined trial.

This point was emphasized by Origenes, one of the greatest church fathers. Preserved in the margin of an ancient manuscript written by a scribe some centuries after his death, is this comment by Origenes on our verse,

"If (one's) life is not 'a being trialled', is not 'a being tempted' (*as a specific initiatory process*), nevertheless that life is not inferior with regard to (*dealing with*) temptation. For comparable to this 'being placed in temptation' (*specifically by spiritual decree*)[48], is to be delivered over (*from within*) to dishonourable desires or to a depraved way of thinking.[49]

Such a person then is in a struggle, conquering neither (*of these two*); but with regard to any such empowered person....(they) are tempted, yet they

---

[48] That is, especially whilst engaging on the spiritual-initiatory path.
[49] In the ancient Grk. πάθη ἀτιμίας ἢ ἀδόκιμον νοῦν

67

do not abandon (the prayer) 'not be placed into temptation'."[50]

Since people generally understand that it cannot be the case that God would bring people into immorality, into the unethical behaviour, and hence be delivered eventually over to evil powers, the meaning of this verse calls out for further clarification. Firstly, we must however, discern a subtle difference between the first three pleas of the lower four. Considering again the first plea, this means in effect,

"May thy influence, in our interface between matter and spirit, daily grant to us a subtler nourishment than material substance for our bodily existence; (a condition which allows us to achieve a harvest for our soul and spirit)."

Here, it is very much a plea to God – or to the veiled spiritual forces in our own soul – that a very mysterious process, far beyond our human 'self' or 'ego' to carry out, does occur. And it is through such a subtle refined nutrient being absorbed, that our consciousness is allowed, whilst we are in the body, to find the link to the deeper purposes and potential of our soul-spiritual being.

Then in the second plea of the four lower pleas, we are requesting the removal of the impact on the world and us, of our more subtle, on-going negative attitudes. For we cannot deal with these energies ourselves directly, but we can grasp that somehow keeping antagonistic and grudge habitual-energies alive, does has a negative effect.

Additionally, we can release our fellow human beings from this. On this basis, the dynamics established through Divine will, and governing the

---

[50] D. Klostermann, *Origenes, Matthäuserklärung: Katenenfragmente* #123, p.64

cosmos, respond quite naturally, in such a way as to remove from us the burden.

With regard to the third plea of these four, "And may Thou not bring us into temptation", this can be translated, when factoring in all the subtle nuances of the Greek as, "May it not be, that you *commence to* bring us into temptation...."

In this third petition or plea, there are two points to observe; one is that the plea is meant to be thought of, like the other pleas, as being made daily. The Greek is in the 'aorist' tense, which indicates that the help from the Divine is a once-off action, not an ongoing, continuous action – so it is limited to that day. The plea is to be renewed each day; hence the Lord's Prayer is intended to be prayed everyday.

Secondly, the Greek here, unlike the three other pleas, uses the 'subjunctive mood', which is the mood of something not definite. Grammatically, the situation here with this plea is quite indefinite, or uncertain. We cannot be sure that we won't be brought into temptation; hence "*may* Thou not..." But because of this, the verse has a futural quality, that is, it looks to the future.

Now this grammatical point is very significant, as it means that this verse is asking that God does not *commence* to bring us into succumbing to our lower desires.[51] In other words, this little Greek phrase of two words, "mae eisenegkaes" (μὴ εἰσενέγκῃς) is in effect saying:

PLEA 6: "May it not be, that you begin to bring us into temptation..."

---

[51] This state of not commencing to do something is called an 'ingressive' quality.

Now we note also that there is a major change in the dynamics of the various petitions. For the first three petitions are beseeching that the Divine becomes a reality in, and for, the developing soul.

The fourth one, (the first of the lower four) is beseeching the Divine to bestow higher, subtler 'food', to assist the physical body's nature to become more refined, or less dense.

The fifth one (the second of the lower four) is beseeching the Divine to spare us from the unpleasant outcome of our habitual, on-going un-spiritual ways of being, by forgiving this. But this can only occur if we, for our part, shall overcome habitual, on-going antipathy to those who have wronged us.

But this sixth petition is specifically beseeching God to *refrain* from bringing us into immoral temptations. That is, we ask God not to debase us. This is a very startling request; this sixth petition is the only one in the Prayer which indicates a possible negative influence of 'God' upon the soul.

A point of entry into trying to understand this very complex and deep theme is that in the Hebrew Scriptures (i.e., the Old Testament), there is a very brief, but equally startling, exact parallel to the plea may God not bring us into temptation.

A similar prayer from the Psalms.
It is in Psalm 141:4 where the Psalmist beseeches God (i.e., Jehovah) not to incline his soul to what is immoral:

> "Do not incline my heart to evil…"
> (NRSV, NEB, KJ, etc.)

This translation is precisely correct to what the Hebrew is saying; the verb here 'natah' (נָתָה) means to incline or pervert or bend, or extend something.

The same startling plea is preserved in the Septuagint's Greek translation of the Hebrew text.[52]

The NRSV has the Hebrew correctly translated, whereas the NIV translation gives the Hebrew verb a different meaning and transfers the action to the heart, instead of God, "Let not my heart be drawn to what is evil". This avoids the very confronting message of the verse.

So what is the implication of this remarkable verse in the Lord's Prayer? As with the other pleas, its focus is the influence of the Creator, working as ferment in Creation through the interweaving of various spirit influences within humanity's inner life. Here it is specifically about the soul of the human, in which evil tendencies are lurking – weakly or strongly – depending upon that person's degree of spirituality. And these unethical qualities have their origin in, and exert an influence on, malignant realms and their associated spirits.

We can only contemplate questions in regard to this over-all theme; specific answers will be elusive. But one query we can have is, whether these malignant energies could have any existence if God had not created circumstances wherein quite possibly, they could come into being. That is, is it possible for a vast life-wave of billions of souls (humanity) which is sharing the cosmos with many, many other life-waves – lowly and noble spiritual beings – to undergo an evolving process throughout Aeons and Ages, without some of them becoming inwardly distant from their Creator?

Any evolutionary process results in some sections of the entities involved moving ahead, and attaining their goals; and others who lag behind

---

[52] Do not incline my heart towards evil things (or motives or words) = μὴ ἐκκλινῃς τὴν καρδιάν μου εἰς λόγπους πονηρίας

and become an obstacle to, or even hostile opponents of, those who have remained in harmony with the Creator's intentions.

This line of thinking leads to the conclusion that the sixth plea is asking that the higher, non-debased influences in Creation from the Divine (or 'God') become active in our consciousness (our soul) with such power that we do not begin to succumb to those other debased, retrograde influences which exist in Creation; for if we do, we become tempted to give in to lower urges.

So taking this larger view of the theme, factoring in humanity's journey through vast evolutionary Ages, we could conclude that the impulses proceeding from God in previous aeons, to commence a complex, many-layered process of evolving many ranks of beings, have resulted in dynamics from which, over the Ages, either evil or good emerged. It is now up to the individual as to what has a predominating presence in one's soul.

Divine beings work with the impulses from God to assist humanity to move towards the good. It could be said that the core Christian teaching is, that through the sacrifice on Golgotha, the cosmic Christ, the leader of the Elohim, is especially present in this immense interweaving.

Verse 13a is a plea that the influence of the cosmic Christ's underlying presence in our soul is strengthened so that our potential for spirituality is empowered. So instead of us starting to succumb daily to the 'lower-self' in a variety of ways, and thus drawing to us malignant influences which have become part of the God-created cosmos, we become subject to the higher, un-fallen influences from the Divine. In this way we empower the higher, nobler potential in us.

This sixth plea is asking that a more consciously directed focus on achieving spirituality prevails in our soul. Also, in contrast to the earlier pleas, this requires us to make concerted effort, in an area where we can certainly make some difference – our own soul life.

By contrast, in the earlier plea about our 'bread' we are indeed asking, with only little capacity to make a difference, that our corporeal nature is able, by absorbing finer ethereal 'nutrient', to assist our consciousness to experience meaning in our existence.

Then the next plea asks for help with the subtle energetic impact of our negative impact upon the community, a dynamic in which we do have a small measure of ability to assist.

In contrast to these, this sixth plea concerns the sphere where we are capable of being involved – and indeed we must actively work towards achieving what we are pleading for. And by the act of praying for non-debased spiritual influences to become active in us, we invoke them.

But this subtle process of allowing divine influences to be active in us occurs through the Grace of Christ; that is, of the cosmic Christ who is declaring these immortal words.

At this point, the contrast of the above considerations to the generally accepted theological view needs to be noted. It is practically universal throughout Christianity that the 'Salvation' of humanity wrought by Christ through the events of Golgotha has given an eternal blessed future to all souls. This is indeed the message presented in many forms in the Pauline epistles.

The conclusion reached by those Christians who have accepted that we do have repeated earth-lives regarding these two different views, is that St. Paul did not wish to present publicly a theology which encompassed the fact of repeated earth-lives. He wrote his epistles in a manner which was in harmony with view that people have but one life. But as a Pharisee he no doubt accepted that reincarnation is a fact; in my *The Gospel of John*, the evidence for this belief being part of ancient Judaism is presented.

Further thoughts about God and evil

It is useful here to consider this confronting theme about the goodness of God, yet the existence of evil in his creation, as understood by a very early Christian teacher; Flavius Clement of Alexandria (AD 150-220). In a passage where he is discussing this topic and the views of esoteric or 'gnostic' Christians about the presence of evil in God's creation, he writes from a deep wisdom;

"...so (we are clear that) nothing occurs without the will of God. Yet this view indeed falls short,[53] in that it is evident that evil things commonly do happen[54], and that God does **not** hinder this.

Yet, this fact alone preserves both the insightfulness regarding the future[55] and the goodness of God. But we are not to imagine that He *brings about* those (evil) sufferings – it is certainly not necessary to think that !

Instead, it is right to be confident that He does not hinder those who are doing this: but, he makes

---

[53] "this (conviction) indeed falls short": I differ here from W. Wilson (1882) and Otto Stählin (1905) who have 'it remains to say that such things happen'. But I view leipetai ('falling short') as referring to the world-view mentioned, not to further explanations.

[54] "commonly happen": for συντομως here is 'readily/commonly', not briefly; and φαιναι here is 'manifesting/occurring', not 'making clear'.

[55] The Grk. word literally means 'prescience'.

serviceable[56] for the Good, the shameless deeds of the Adversary."(*Stromateis*, Bk.4:12)

                                                          trans. the author

This last sentence is from a profound observation of life; that the outcome of the soul encountering or manifesting anti-social behaviour is mostly that, stirred by our conscience, we become more determined to bring goodness and compassion into our world. This, Clement teaches, is an indicator of God's foresight regarding the future that awaits us, and his goodness in arranging that this dynamic arises in the soul, enabling us to eventually leave evil behind.

Rudolf Steiner's research into the dynamics enveloping the human life-wave on its journey, shows that there would be no evil entities, no debased forms of spirit, if God had not brought about an evolutionary dynamic of vast proportions, encompassing millions and millions of years, in which of necessity a possibility for evil arises amongst the vast numbers of spirit beings.

That is, there naturally arises either a hasty yearning towards an indulgent self-centred unrealistic goal; towards goals that are not yet possible, and hence goals that are not 'God-willed'. Or there can emerge a hardened, isolationist, self-centred determination to gain power over others.

Such disharmonious tendencies nurture influences from spirits that are self-focussed – and thus not in harmony with the intentions of the Godhead. These dynamics then reverberate into the souls of human beings.

---

[56] makes serviceable": viewing καταχρῆσθαι as a verbal form of the noun καταχρησις (make serviceable), and not from the verb καταχραομαι, though the two words are closely associated.

This challenging reality is the theme of the *Book of Job* which presents the story of Satan tempting Job. It is startling to read in the introduction to this text, that as various of the hierarchical deities gather for the equivalent of an earthly conference with Jahve, Satan is quite welcome, and his normal location is revealed as the interior of the Earth,

"One day the sons of the Elohim came to present themselves to Jahve, and Satan also came amongst them. The Lord said to Satan, "Where have you come from?" Satan answered the Lord, "From going to and fro in the Earth, and from walking up and down in[57] it."

As in well known, Jahve then gives Satan the opportunity to attack Job morally. An invaluable insight into this esoteric, cosmic view of evil is given in the priceless ancient Coptic text, *Codex Askew* or *Codex Pistis Sophia*, which preserves teachings of the risen Jesus to his disciples. The section from Chapter 45 is addressing an evil deity,

> "you are only....a being which has not offered up what has been purified of its light, that it may be saved. Instead such an entity (*blindly*) boasts of the abundant radiance of its (own) being, for it did not emanate forth anything (into the cosmos, for other beings) from the power which was in itself."

Here we learn that a malignant entity is described as one which is enabled by some of the dynamics underlying the cosmos, to selfishly hold onto its own power - instead of offering up this to the higher Divine Being, thereby letting this light permeate other beings.

---

[57] "in the Earth': modern translations have 'on the Earth' but the Heb. preposition (בְּ) also means 'in'.

Such an entity is directly opposing the core principle of God, and of the divine gods: that is, a selfless giving over of one's own spiritual light so that thereby other spirits can be nourished.

Other passages in the Pistis Sophia codex reveal the initiatory Christian understanding, as taught by the risen Jesus, in the first decade of the new religion, that 'God' permits evil powers to exert their influences on humanity. In Chapter 47 the suffering Pistis Sophia entity is only assisted by the cosmic Christ after 'God' has given a command to that effect; "However, the commandment of the First Mystery was not yet fulfilled for her repentance to be accepted..." And in Chapter 58, "I sent this (light) down into the Chaos, until the command should come from the First Mystery to take Pistis Sophia entirely out of the Chaos."

In Chapter 64 she is only finally rescued from the attacks of satanic powers after 'God' (who is called *the First Mystery*) gives the command to that effect. The theological implications here are profound; as in the *Book of Job*, evil spirits may indeed bring about suffering and horrors, for this is an unavoidable dynamic in Creation, and as such can be viewed as 'permitted' by God. As Jesus himself taught, it is necessary that evil exists, but woe to those through whom it comes (Matt.18:7).

So, this petition in the Lord's Prayer is signifying that through praying or beseeching that our soul may be aligned to the Good, a dynamic is set in motion for divine influences from God to become stronger within us.

Considering the potent cosmic truth here, some profound words from Rudolf Steiner are relevant: he was referring to deities who are regressive or fallen (known as 'luciferic gods') and thus incite unethical behaviour. He taught that this phenomenon, wherein some deities are remaining behind (in their potential to be divine, and thus lead humans into evil) has a very good aspect to it.

He states, "This is true in so far as it is the experience of evil by humanity that becomes the primary impelling influence in human souls, via the conscience, to then reject evil and move forward morally towards the Good; ...all things, whether those progressing forwards, or those regressing, are both of a divine nature (as to their origin)."[58]

This very potent, challenging point, that divine and also malignant influences are all part of the reality of God's creation, is what Clement of Alexandria is saying, while emphasizing that the will of God shall transform unethical qualities into good.

A similar perspective underlies a brief answer from Rudolf Steiner to a question about this sixth plea - of being tempted - after a lecture in 1912. He replied,

"May the divine kernel within me not be active in such a way that I fall into temptation; (but instead) may this divine kernel so strengthen my inner spiritual nature (not my fallen unethical qualities), that I may avoid the temptation."[59]

We begin to see, as a brief answer to our query, that the sincere yearning for enhanced spirituality results in the Divine having a more powerful presence within us, thus in that very second when a temptation starts to impact upon the soul, it is rejected.

---

[58] GA 101, lect. 24st March 1908.
[59] In GA 92 p. 397. Personal notes were taken by someone unknown of his words, such notes are often faulty; (the next sentence of the answer is defective).

Now, with regard to the sixth plea, we are faced with the question, how do we ensure that the Divine is made active in us towards spiritualizing our being, and that we do not become exposed to an influence which takes us into the experience of further ethical failures.

We need to answer the question, how do we not start to succumb to temptation; how do ensure the impulses towards the good are active in us? Help in answering this is to be found in a profound verse from Rudolf Steiner. His beautiful meditation on the Lord's Prayer - published in my *The Way to the Sacred* - allows us to lift our understanding of the Lord's Prayer to a deeply intuitive level. Here is my translation of that meditation:

"Our Father, Thou who wert and are
and shall be,
our very innermost being.
Thy being is glorified and praised by all of us.
May Thy kingdom be extended by our deeds and our conduct.
We fulfil Thy will as Thou, O Father, hast placed it in our innermost soul.
The nourishment of the spirit, the Bread of Life,
Thou givest in abundance to us, in all the changing conditions of life.
Thou allowest not temptation to come upon us beyond our strength,
for in Thy being no temptation can exist.
Because the Tempter is only illusion and deception,
out of which Thou, O Father, leads us through
the light of Thy cognition.
Thy power and glory is efficacious within us in
all the ages of the cycles of time.
Amen".

There is much insight in particular from these words;

> Thou allowest not temptation to come upon us beyond our strength,
> for in Thy being no temptation can exist.
> Because the Tempter is only illusion and deception,
> out of which Thou, O Father, leadest us through the light of Thy cognition.

This final part of the sentence is in effect saying that a person who does so pray - in this deeper esoteric sense - is in effect someone who is striving to bring the presence of God, or the efficacy of the Divine, (the interweaving of the divine hierarchies) into one's consciousness, in an empowered condition.

In other words, in the developing Spiritual-self, influences from the divine spirits, such as Angels and Archangels, as mediators of divine higher beings, become efficacious. (Naturally, many whose heart-wisdom is truly deep can also achieve this, without having a spiritual awareness; that is a conscious awareness of the specific esoteric dynamics involved.)

In the developing Spiritual-self, the cognitional capacity is ennobled; divine wisdom now has some subtle presence in one's soul-life. The veiled divinity - in effect 'God' - has started to become present within the person, and this awakening of divine reality for the person, grants the capacity to perceive a temptation and enable the person to then rightly assess and reject it, before it becomes a threat.

The previously unconscious human bearer of the Divine is becoming merged consciously with the Divine - and through the "light of Its cognition" we are "led out of the illusion and deception".

"only illusion and deception": as the process of sensing a temptation occurring, the person seeking spiritual wisdom becomes aware just how illusory, false and unethical is that temptation. It is not that the tempting spirit is an illusion, but that its influences create a host of shallow or self-centred yearnings and attitudes.

SEVENTH PLEA: 13b:
Correlates to: our sense of 'I'; or 'the ego'

"but instead, draw us away from evil."
This is usually "...**but, deliver us from evil.**"
(ἀλλὰ ῥῦσαι ἡμᾶς ἀπὸ τοῦ πονηροῦ)

We shall now consider the last part of the Lord's Prayer. It now follows very organically from the above considerations, that verse 13b is indeed the last part of the Prayer, for verse 13b applies to the ego, or self. The verse is grammatically ambiguous, and hence could also be translated as
"...but, deliver us from the Evil One."

However, this is surely not what is meant, because the meaning intended by Christ follows on from the first part of the sentence. This first part, 13a, is about the soul having the possibility of falling into unethical temptations. Hence the next concern – in 13b – of our prayer, concerns our self, or ego; namely that it does not as a consequence, become guilty of evil, of committing evil deeds.

Now, the verb used here 'hruomai' (ῥύομαι) doesn't simply mean to 'deliver', 'rescue' or 'save'; its history goes back to Classical Greek times when it arose from the verb 'heruoe' (ῥύω), which in addition to 'rescue' and 'save', means 'to be set free', 'to be drawn ashore', 'to drag' (away from).

This nuance of being saved or delivered, by being *drawn away* from evil, is deliberately implied here.

The same verse in an expanded translation, giving its inner meaning....

" but instead, draw us (our ego) **away from evil."**

It is one thing for the soul to be tempted; it is another thing when the person, their 'I', actually carries out an unethical deed.

These words from Rudolf Steiner give a valuable over-all perspective on the sevenfold Prayer: "When a human being goes through life determined to spiritualize themselves by using the four lower pleas as a guide, then through doing this, that person begins to develop the three higher stages of their human nature."[60]

One needs to note here that such an intention in an acolyte actually starts out in a very mysterious way; the Holy Spirit's ever-present wish to bring about such a search for a path to holiness in the human heart is the actual origin of this search to become, as it were, spiritually 're-born'.

---

[60] In GA 100, lect. of 21st June, 1907.

THE LORD'S PRAYER:
Matthew 6: 9-13

Our Father, Thou in the Heavens,

Let Thy name be sanctified

Let Thy Kingdom draw near

Let Thy will come into being:

As in Heaven, so upon the Earth.

Give to us daily our bread:
'bread' above physical substance,
'bread' which offers itself up to us

And forgive us our moral debts,
as we also forgive those who become indebted to us,

and, may Thou not bring us into temptation

but, draw us away from evil.

For Thine is the Power, the Kingdom and the Glory, forever and ever; amen.

PART TWO

The prayer in the Gospel of Luke (11:2-4)
"Father,
Let Thy name be sanctified
Let Thy kingdom draw near
Be giving to us day by day our bread,
the bread above physical substance,
and forgive us our sins,
for indeed we ourselves are forgiving
all those indebted to us,
and may Thou not bring us into temptation."

It is a wide-spread understanding that in Luke's Gospel, there is an incomplete version of the Lord's Prayer. That is, four of the nine lines of the complete Prayer, are apparently missing – as compared to the Lord's Prayer in Matthew's Gospel.

However, there are ancient versions of the Gospels (made of vellum[61]) in which the Prayer in Luke's Gospel is larger, having several lines added to it; these were borrowed by scribes from the Prayer in Matthew's Gospel. These valuable books with the larger prayer are dated from about AD 390 to 450. They are discussed below.

But there are also two other ancient books in which the Prayer in Luke is as we find it in today's Bibles; that is shorter, looking like an incomplete Lord's Prayer. So there is confusion as to whether the Luke prayer was a different version of the Lord's Prayer. This confusion prevailed already in the fourth century, as displayed by these earliest formal versions of the New Testament. To sort out this problem, let's review what were the earliest great New Testament books.

---

[61] vellum is thin animal skin, much superior to papyrus.

There are in existence, four great ancient, bound books (called codices) of the Bible:

Codex **Sinaiticus** : about AD 350
  almost all of the Bible

codex **Vaticanus**: about AD 350
  was complete, but some pages has been lost

codex **Alexandrinos**: about AD 350
  was complete, only very few pages lost

codex **Ephraemi Syrii**: about AD 450
  damaged, was complete, some pages lost

But I add to these four:
codex **Bezae**: about AD 450
It has only the Gospels and some of Acts: but its text often preserves more accurate esoteric versions of the Gospel words.

and also:
The **Freer** codex[62]: about AD 400
contains the four Gospels only

Now to these six documents can be added a seventh ancient and valuable text; **Papyrus #75**. It is a papyrus folio from about AD 175-200. I include it here because it pre-dates the above books by about 200-300 years, and is the only very early text which does contain most of Luke's Gospel.

Now of these seven documents, three contain the well-known short prayer which is understood to be an incomplete version of the Lord's Prayer in Luke. But the other four record a long version in Luke's Gospel, which was created by borrowing from the Lord's Prayer in Matthew's Gospel.

---

[62] Also known as the Washington Manuscript.

The short prayer is in: **Sinaiticus, Vaticanus** and **papyrus 75**.
A long version of this prayer, with verses borrowed from the Lord's Prayer, is in: **Bezae, Alexandrinos, Freer** and **Ephraemi Syrii**.

So, about a century after the three earlier ancient books were made, some other versions of Luke's Gospel, now had the apparently 'complete' Lord's Prayer in Luke's gospel. This situation presented a challenge to scholars. What was going on?

Did those books with the 'short' prayer, represent a corrupted version of Luke's Gospel, which should always have had the 'complete' Prayer in it? Or was the 'incomplete' version the true original; so did Matthew make up the additional verses and add them to his account of the Prayer?

Scholars have concluded that the people who compiled those four impressive books from about AD 400-450: Freer, Bezae, Alexandrinus, Ephraemi Syrii - decided to transfer from the Gospel of Matthew into their books, the rest of the Lord's Prayer into Luke's Gospel. They obviously did this because they felt that this Prayer should not left incomplete. I agree with the conclusion that scribes decided to add verses into the Luke Gospel prayer.

Other scholars have decided however, that actually the 'incomplete' version of Luke's Gospel is the oldest text we have, and is the true version of the Lord's Prayer. These scholars concluded that Matthew decided to create the additional four verses found in his Gospel. But, as you will know from Part One of this booklet, this is an erroneous view.

Here is what we can conclude about the situation: the prayer in Luke's Gospel **is not** the Lord's Prayer.

All the discussion about this theme, over many centuries, has been following a false trail. For there were two different prayers given by Jesus; and these prayers were given in very different circumstances.

As we saw in Part One, the actual Lord's Prayer was the highest, most sublime part of the teachings which the cosmic Christ, through Jesus, intoned in Devachan, in the presence of the 12 Disciples, whose consciousness was lifted to that level. (As we noted on p.8)

But in Luke's Gospel, the place and circumstances are entirely different. Jesus had selected 72 people from his many followers, to become closer to him, to become in effect, disciples. Now in reading the introduction in Luke's Gospel to the event, one needs to know that the Greek word for 'disciple' (mathaetaes - μαθητής) also meant 'follower' or 'adherent':

"One day Jesus was praying in a certain place. When he had finished, one of his followers said to him, "Lord, teach us to pray, just as John (*the Baptist*) taught his disciples."

So here Jesus and the special 12 Disciples have not raised their consciousness into the heavenly realms. What Luke is recording is an earthly event, and the prayer which Jesus then gives is not a sublime cosmic intoning; it has a much less cosmic quality, and as such, is understandable to any sincere follower. This is affirmed when the Greek text is carefully experienced. So when clearly understood, the introductory words should read, "...one of his *followers* said to him, "Lord.."

The prayer given to the un-named follower is:

1 "Father,
2 Let Thy name be sanctified

3 Let Thy kingdom draw near
4 Be giving to us day by day our bread,
 the bread above physical substance,
5 and forgive us our sins,
 for indeed we ourselves are forgiving
 all those indebted to us,
6 and may Thou not bring us into temptation."

The different nature of this prayer
in line 1: God is not 'our Father' and he is not specified as being located in the Heavens.
Lines 2 and 3: it was a definite feature of prayers of the Hebrew people, that they prayed for any reference to God to be regarded as referring to a very sacred being. Also, they prayed for God's kingdom to become a reality on the Earth, restoring Israel's reality which had been devastated by the forced removal of the Hebrew people to foreign lands.

This may be how that follower of Jesus understood these words, in his cultural-religious context. However, these same two lines could also be understood in the deeper way that we have explained in Part One.

Line 4: "Be giving to us day by day our bread..."
but in the great cosmic Prayer the plea is: "Give to us *daily* our bread...". This version places more emphasis upon receiving the subtle nutrition as we actually eat our food, today.

Line 5a: "forgive us our sins": the actual Lord's Prayer has "forgive us our (moral) debts" and is thereby referring to the long-term habitual lack of harmony in us to what is godly; as well as to darkly brooding, long-term ill-will. As we noted in Part One, this occurs in the ether around us. But the word 'sin' placed here avoids that profound theme.

Line 5b: "...for indeed we ourselves are forgiving all those..." This contrasts to the Prayer in Matthew, "as we also forgive those who are indebted to us..." So here the prayer in Luke's Gospel presents a substantially different plea. For with the cosmic Lord's Prayer there is a condition imposed: if 'God' (i.e, the divinely established processes in spiritual realms governing human existence) is to forgive the human being's habitual un-spiritual ways of being, then that human being must make the inner effort to forgive a person or persons who have been, for some time, injuring them. It is a question of removing simmering ill-will from the ethers.

But with the lesser, more individual prayer, as recorded in Luke, this required condition is absent. Instead, the devout follower declares boldly that he certainly is forgiving all and sundry: "...for indeed we ourselves are forgiving all those...". The person praying like this, is in effect both certifying this to be a fact, and encouraging themselves to be kind-hearted generally.

Line 6: the same as in the Lord's Prayer

So, superfluous to this version are:
 "Our (*Father*), the one in the Heavens..."

Here God is not so directly identified as the Father of all the individual people.

And also this line:

 "Let Thy will come into being..."

For here in the Lord's Prayer, as noted in Part One, the plea is that the extraordinary heights of initiatory spirituality may be achieved wherein the otherwise immeasurably deep and vast Will of the Father-God, a reflection of which lies deeply veiled and disempowered in the normal human will, starts to become a tangible presence in the initiate.

And also this line was not needed:

"As in Heaven, so upon the Earth"

This line in the Lord's Prayer has a cosmic dimension to it; it refers to the potential blossoming of all three spiritual potentials in the human spirit: the Spiritual-self, the divine life-forces (or Life-spirit) and the divine will (or Spirit-human).

As such, it transcends the scope of the yearnings which a private individual prayer can be expected to encompass.

Finally, the last line of the Lord's Prayer, "but draw us away from evil", had no place in the other prayer; the one given to this unnamed follower.

For the purposes of a personal prayer, this additional plea was apparently considered by Jesus as not necessary, for it is implied in the preceding line: "bring us not into temptation". But it is essential for a full correlation of the sevenfold Prayer to the sevenfold human being. This is what makes the Lord's Prayer so sublime.

Those seven ancient documents mentioned above are generally all of high quality, that is, reliable texts. However, the expert committee led by professors K & B Aland, who in the mid-to-late 20 century, created the definitive Greek NT, do regard codex Vaticanus as of higher quality, more reliable, than parts of codex Alexandrinos.

Consequently, the now almost universally used authoritative Greek NT book – *The Greek New Testament* – presents what people have incorrectly defined as the short version of the Lord's Prayer in

Luke's gospel; not the longer Lord's Prayer as found in Matthew's Gospel.

This has also been the case for centuries in the western world. In 1516 the great Dutch scholar Erasmus studied various ancient Greek texts, and wrote to many scholars in the course of his work to enable him to eventually produce a definitive Greek New Testament. He used the copies of Luke's Gospel which have the 'shorter version', that is not the Lord's Prayer.

The text from Erasmus became the major factor influencing the translation made by Martin Luther in Germany and by William Tyndale in England, in their efforts to produce an accurate Bible in the language of their people.

This is a good outcome for all Bible students, as we now can be clear that the Gospel of Luke does actually contain a different, short prayer, which is not what is universally known as 'the Lord's Prayer'. So it is clear the three other codices which have the long version in Luke's Gospel are the result of scribes adding in the "missing" verses, borrowed from the Gospel of Matthew.

'Let Thy Holy Spirit come upon us...'
We have seen that the Gospel of Luke does not contain the Lord's Prayer – not in full, and not abbreviated either. It contains a different prayer given on a different occasion by Jesus.

But there is another misunderstanding about the Lord's Prayer in relation to the other prayer in Luke's Gospel. Some scholars have concluded that the plea, "Let Thy kingdom come" is not the true, original version. They think that the original plea in the Gospel of Luke and in Matthew's Gospel was 'Let Thy Holy Spirit come upon us and purify us'.

But the definitive Greek New Testament book produced by a team led by Professors A. and B. Aland ignores this alternative version, and retains 'May thy kingdom come'. So what is the situation here?

The only Gospel of Luke edition to contain this alternative version is that created by the heretic Marcion, who in AD 144 founded his own Christian church. Marcion was not a reliable, careful scholar. He decided that only the Gospel of Luke was valid; so he dismissed the Gospel of Matthew, Mark and John from his work. But he also decided to delete the Nativity story in Luke, and to change various verses in the Gospel which did not suit his ideas. He also adopted just some of the Epistles, and even changed their wording where it suited him.

As part of this editorial activity, he created the alternative version of the prayer in Luke, 'May Thy Holy Spirit come and purify us'. Some researchers think that Marcion was incorporating these words here because they are the genuine, original version, and not an alternative version created by Marcion.

However, the majority of scholars, including myself, do not share this view; the reason for this shall become clear as we proceed. One example supporting the majority conclusion is that a contemporary of Marcion, called Justin Martyr, who was an ardent defender of the newly developing Christian religion in a hostile world, severely attacks Marcion. In his writings, Justin quotes from the actual Gospel of Luke. In addition to the four accepted, validated Gospels, Justin also had access to the altered, truncated New Testament created by Marcion.

However, Justin does not even mention this alternative verse in Luke, as presented in Marcion's text. To Justin, it was obviously not even worth discussing, just another part of the falsification of Luke's Gospel carried out by Marcion.

Marcion was determined to portray the God of the Old Testament as hostile to the God that Jesus refers to. An example of the unwholesome nature of Marcion's view is to be found in his alteration of a verse in the Epistle to the Ephesians (3:9). This states in a correct translation,
"...to enlighten all people concerning the stewardship of the Mystery having been hidden in God – the one who created all things."

But Marcion changes "*in* God, the one who..." to "*from* the God who created all things..."

So in his Gospel this reads,
"...to enlighten all people concerning the stewardship of the Mystery having been hidden from God – the one who created all things."

In other words, the creator of the visible world was a dubious deity, greatly inferior to the true God.

The only known Gospel text to have this alternative plea, "May Thy Holy Spirit come and purify us", is Marcion's own corrupted Gospel of Luke.[63]

But confusion around this plea intensified through the emerging of another distinctive group of Christians in the second century. These were the Montanists, whose leader, Montanos, put strong emphasis on the Holy Spirit as a very important divine being, whom he hoped would and could, directly inspire himself and others in his movement. Montanism had a precarious existence in the early church, approved by some, but disapproved of by others. It was not viewed as a heresy, rather as a specific, unusual grouping

---

[63] Luke's Gospel does emphasize the Holy Spirit, which is probably why Marcion chose it as the 'valid' Gospel.

within the church, until the fourth century when laws were passed against them.

A second century African church writer, Tertullian (approx. AD 160-215) became an ardent supporter of Montanism, and in one text about the prayer in Luke's Gospel he infers that the Holy Spirit should be approached fervently by Christians; "Of whom can I ask for His (*God's*) Holy Spirit"[64].

However here Tertullian does not quote the Marcion alternative verse, but he is obviously thinking of this. He also does not state that this alternative verse is in the Lord's Prayer. This situation would have been awkward for Tertullian, since he wrote vehemently against the Marcionites.

It is known that Tertullian did not find Marcion's alternative verse for the prayer convincing, for in his substantial essay *On Prayer*, in which he refers to the Lord's Prayer in detail, he ignores the Marcion version. Tertullian only began to make vague references to the Holy Spirit in regard to the prayer, when he became interested in the Montanists.

Now the historical context needs to be noted; as from the fourth century, Christianity became an officially tolerated religion, no longer suppressed. Consequently more and more church fathers could write and travel, teaching their faith, developing their theology. Since many Christians were attracted to the teachings of Montanos, this meant that Montanism also grew.

We mentioned earlier that this alternative verse in the Lukan prayer has survived in only two late manuscripts from the 11th and 12th centuries. So in all the many New Testament versions produced as from the fourth century, this verse is not found.

---

[64] Tertullian, *Against Marcion*, 4:26.

The church, which around the fourth and fifth centuries, was now allowed and no longer suppressed by the secular authorities, decided to produce expensive, impressive Christian Bibles, to in effect proclaim what was the 'canon'; that is the officially recognized Scriptures.

These are the books, called a codex, which we discussed earlier; that is, Sinaiticus, Vaticanus and Alexandrinos. But one can include codex Bezae, and also the Freer manuscript. In none of these books, was this alternative verse placed in the altered Gospel of Luke from Marcion incorporated.

In fact, already in the second century it was not included in the great papyrus text, Papyrus no. 75, written about 50 years after Marcion founded his church.

However, the situation became confusing when such an alternative verse was referred to, some two centuries later in the writings of Gregory of Nyssa a prominent fourth century church Father (AD 330-395).

Gregory writes, "For so says Luke in his Gospel; instead of 'Thy Kingdom come', it reads, "May Thy Holy Spirit come upon us and purify us…..for what Luke calls 'the Holy Spirit', Matthew calls 'the Kingdom'… "[65]

What Gregory does here through a play on words, is trying to reconcile those with a Montanist inclination to the now prevailing Orthodox Church.

He is saying that 'Kingdom' can be viewed as having more or less the same meaning as 'Holy Spirit'. He can allege this because the Greek word for 'kingdom', which is 'basileia', has two meanings:

---

[65] Gregory of Nyssa, *De Oratione* (*The Lord's Prayer*) sermon 3.

'kingdom' or 'kingship' (that is, sovereignty, regal power). The Holy Spirit can be thought of as an empowered, 'regal' deity.

Gregory then comments that Luke, (in this other unorthodox version) is in effect invoking the empowered, sovereign Holy Spirit, who has a central role in the Kingdom of God.

The Holy Spirit was considered to be such an empowered deity by theologians throughout the history of the church, before Gregory and long after him. It is understood to be the instrument through which the kingdom of God is made manifest.

When we analyse the context of his comments, the situation becomes clearer. Firstly, this is not the same as what Marcion created; for the plea that Gregory quotes replaces the verse, 'May thy kingdom come'; it is not in the first line, as it was with Marcion.

But we need to acknowledge that it is at first puzzling that Gregory even mentions this, because he was selected to be a defender of mainstream church theology of his time. In fact, Emperor Theodosius gave him access to imperial post-horses and carriages to assist him to travel to areas where doctrinal differences were creating social divisions.[66]

It is also striking to recall that while Gregory was writing this, codex Sinaiticus and codex Vaticanus were being created by the mainstream church. These two authoritative books were designed to present and confirm the authentic New Testament canon, now that the church was free of state persecution. In these two, the alternative verse in Luke is not incorporated.

---

[66] Butler's *Lives of the Saints*: for March 9th.

A key to this odd situation is found in the fact that Gregory worked extensively to reconcile various divisive groups arising in the church. Gregory was the brother of St. Basil the Great, and both were highly regarded in the church. As part of his reconciliation work of combating heretical tendencies in the churches, Gregory was sent to Armenia, Palestine and Arabia.

Whilst Gregory was carrying out his reconciliation endeavours, his brother Basil had stated his antipathy formally to the misuse of the role of the Holy Spirit by the various heretical groups still operative in Christendom. He specifies the Valentinians[67], Manichaeans, Marcionites[68] and Montanists in his first canonical Epistle to a fellow priest, Amphilochus; "I consider of no value the baptism of the Pepuzenes (*i.e., Montanists*), and I am puzzled that Dionysos the Canonist was of a different view....such heresies make people alien to the Faith...they who baptize into the Father, Son and Montanos – or Priscilla[69] – sin against the Holy Spirit."[70]

Returning now to Gregory quoting this alternative verse:
"For so says Luke in his Gospel; instead of 'Thy Kingdom come', it reads, "May Thy Holy Spirit come upon us and purify us…"

---

[67] Still existing until ca. 400 – although these Gnostics were probably no longer truly echoing the world-view of Valentinos.
[68] Substantial numbers of these heretics were still being converted back to the church in AD 458 by Theodoret, Bishop of Cyprus.
[69] She was a very senior Montanist.
[70] From, *The First Canonical Epistle of our holy Father Basil, Archbishop of Caesarea in Cappadocia, to Amphilochus Bishop of Iconium*,
(www.orthodoxchurchfathers.com)

It appears to me that it was an integral aspect of his reconciliation work that led him to mention this. Gregory believed this text derived from some (spurious) alternative version of Luke's Gospel. This alternative version was, I conclude, a Montanist version of Luke's Gospel.

I conclude that a Montanist Christian scribe had copied out the Gospel of Luke and incorporated the Holy Spirit verse into the prayer, either directly or as a marginal note.

For under no circumstances would Gregory have used in his arguments a text from Marcion, the despised heretic. But he could have used a text from the Montanist movement, and for good reason. For this would have been a conciliatory act to the now forbidden, frustrated Montanist Christians.

The repression of the Montanists began when Gregory was a child, and by the time of Gregory's work, they were no longer tolerated; no doubt resulting in a large pool of discontented ex-Montanists. So Gregory was attempting to reconcile these Montanists with the church, by the risky decision to quote from some altered version of the Gospel of Luke.

MAXIMUM CONFESSOR
This same alternative verse which Gregory used is also mentioned about 200 years later, by another prominent church official, Maximum the Confessor (AD 580-662). It appears that Maximus was making use of Gregory's text. Maximus writes,
"...the kingdom of God the Father exists in 'substantial form' (*i.e., tangible form*) as the Holy Spirit. What Matthew calls 'the Kingdom' in this context, one of the other Evangelists has elsewhere

called the 'Holy Spirit', saying, "May Thy Holy Spirit come upon us."[71]

Before this paragraph Maximus had been explaining that the 'Kingdom of the Father' is in effect a condition in us, in which the Holy Spirit is present and active. He comments,

"...for having done away anger and desire, we are now made into a temple for God through the Holy Spirit by the teaching and practise of gentleness".

It is not possible that Maximus made a supporting reference to his convictions by using the version from the despised Marcion. The solution to this situation is that he is using the writings of Gregory of Nyssa. Maximus probably did not have access to the altered version of the Luke Gospel which Gregory had before him. This would account for the very vague words of Maximus..."one of the other evangelists has elsewhere called 'the Holy Spirit' what Mathew calls 'the Kingdom'."

In any event, Maximus wants to emphasize the central role of the Holy Spirit in Christian life; he is not focussing on just what verse was in Luke's Gospel.

The significant point here is that Maximus was, like Gregory, also a prominent defender of mainstream church theology against divisive ideas and heresies. It is reported that Maximus had the view that 'the smallest theological point was to be affirmed at the risk of one's life'.[72] So Maximus would not have quoted from Marcion's edited Gospel.

Summarizing this historical record of references to the alternative verse:

---

[71] Maximus, *On the Lord's Prayer*.
[72] The Catholic Encyclopaedia, *Maximus of Constantinople*, Vol. 10, p. 79.

in the second century Tertullian indirectly implies this alternative verse is compatible with the Lord's Prayer, but does not specifically say the alternative verse as in it, (despite some claims to the contrary). Also papyrus 75, written in this same century, does not include this alternative verse.

Then in the fourth century, Gregory affirms this alternative verse, no doubt because of its attraction to Montanists, but in the same century the very substantial and reliable codices – Sinaiticus and Vaticanus – and the Freer codex, were created as a definitive text for the now permitted church; yet these do not incorporate it.

Then in the sixth-seventh century, Maximus affirms it; yet already in the fifth century, the great codices Bezae and Alexandrinus were compiled, as well as the Ephraemi Syrii texts. These writings also did not incorporate this alternative version.

Moreover, this alternative version is not present in any other ancient manuscript. It is only found in two very late (medieval) Greek manuscripts as noted earlier; dating from the 11th and 12th centuries, that is, mss. 604 (changed to #700) and mss. #162. These have "Let thy Holy Spirit come upon us, and purify us" instead of either 'Thy kingdom come' or instead of 'Hallowed be thy name'.

So I conclude that Gregory had a version of Luke's Gospel which had been altered by Montanists; and Maximus later made use of Gregory's comments. So an altered (falsified) copy Luke's Gospel had circulated amongst a small group of people, on the edge of the general Christian church. Whilst the accurate version circulated amongst a much larger number of Christians.

It is helpful here to emphasize again that Luke's Gospel did not originally have the verse "Let the

Holy Spirit come upon us". This is only found in the gospel version created by Marcion; and he was obviously someone who would delete or alter any part of Scripture that he did not agree with; and also add words that underpinned his distorted view of Christianity.

Although in the fourth century Gregory of Nyssa, who lived much later than Marcion, did refer to a document which seems similar to what Marcion produced. Except that in the text Gregory had, the verse replaced the words, 'Let Thy kingdom come', whereas with Marcion it was placed in the first line. This was created no doubt by a Montanist scribe. More evidence exists that this alternative verse was concocted by Marcion.

Tertullian
We can note again that Tertullian as a Montanist, writing just a few decades after Marcion, would have eagerly greeted such a verse in the Lord's Prayer. But he knew of no such text in the authentic Gospel. This is a very significant fact considering that Tertullian knew Marcion's writings, which he vehemently opposed.

Justin Martyr
Justin Martyr, a contemporary of Marcion, who knew the four canonical Gospels as well as Marcion's work, ignored this verse, despite quoting from Luke's Gospel in his own writings. So we can conclude the Justin regarded the Marcion verse as spurious.

The Didache
In addition, that very early document (dated to AD 50 or AD 70-80) summing up the core of Christian teachings, called the 'Didache', included the Lord's Prayer as found in the Gospel of Matthew. But the Prayer in this text does not include the verse about the Holy Spirit.

Origenes
Finally, there is the response of the great theologian, Origenes of Alexandria, one of the very greatest theologians in church history. He was an outstanding scholar, who gathered up various versions of New Testament Scriptures; he did not restrict himself to just one version of a Gospel. For example, in his *Commentary on Mathew's Gospel* he writes, "Matthew then, according to some of the documents, has written...." (book 12, para. 15).

Origenes was of course familiar with the Luke Gospel and other Scriptural texts produced by Marcion. Like Tertullian and others, Origenes treated the unprincipled editing of the Gospel by Marcion as worse than just irrelevant. For Origenes was writing about AD 220 and had very early copies of genuine Scriptural texts, no doubt this included Luke's Gospel.

As a revered master of Christian teachings with a large library, Origenes' copies of the Gospels and Epistles would have been of excellent quality; these could well have been copied only a few decades after the original Gospels were written.

Of Luke's Gospel, he writes, referring to Marcion's version of this Gospel, "I conclude Marcion took sound words in a wrong sense when he rejected Jesus' birth from Mary, and declared ..."

Consequently, in his treatise *On Prayer* (*de Oratione*) Origenes discusses the Lord's Prayer in detail, without any reference to the words about the Holy Spirit to be found in Marcion's version of Luke's Gospel.

It is a consequence of all these historical facts, that the definitive Greek New Testament, developed by the Committee led by K. and B. Aland in the late 20th century, quite correctly does not recognize as valid a verse about the Holy Spirit, in the prayer in Luke's Gospel.

The Doxology
This term is used to describe the beautiful ritualistic words added after the end of the Prayer: "For Thine is the Kingdom, the Power and the Glory, forever and ever, amen."

These words are not included in the Greek New Testament as developed by the group led by K. and B. Aland. Although they are included in older translations, such as the King James, and Martin Luther Bible (Die Bibel), they are omitted in the NIV and NRSV, for example.

This is because Erasmus, in developing his Greek New Testament text in 1516, (known as the Textus Receptus) included the doxology. Because of this it was consequently used by Martin Luther in his German translation of the New Testament (in 1522) and then by the King James Bible translators (in 1611).

The situation here is that these words are included in some of the old manuscripts from the 3rd to 5th centuries; but omitted in others.

See the next page where this historical situation is set out in a clear tabular form.

Tracing the Use of the Doxology

Century	YES – in the L-P	NO – not in the L-P
1st	Didache	
2nd	Diatessaron	quoted by Tertullian
3rd	Curet. Syriac	Sinait. Syriac
4th- 5th	Alexandrinos Freer mss. Peshitta one Old Latin	Sinaiticus Vaticanus Bezae Veronensis[73] Vercellensis Dublinensis
9th	about 10 have it	no others have it
	Church Fathers used	**Church Fathers not used**
2nd		Tertullian
3rd		Origenes, Cyprian
4-5th	Chrysostom	Augustine

We see that only a minority of ancient texts have this doxology; and that the great Origenes and other early theologians did not comment on it.

---

[73] Veronensis & Vercellensis are the 2 oldest Latin mss. of the Gospels known (4th century)

The Lord's Prayer as written in the earliest Gospel books

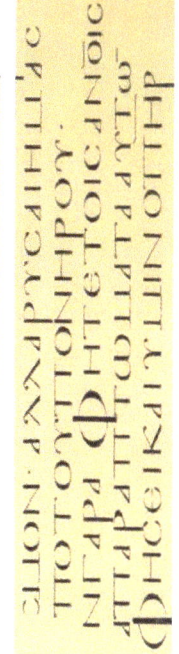

above L: Freer codex ca. AD 400
above R: Vaticanus codex ca. 350
Oppos: Alexandrinos codex ca.450
below L: from the Vercellensis codex ca.375, (set in readable typescript); it has the earliest Latin Gospels

```
so et pater tuus            ta nostra sicut et
qui uidet in abs            [nos] debitoribus nostris
conso reddet             13 et ne nos inducas
tibi in palam.              in temptatio
Orantes autem               nem sed libe
nolite multu                ra nos a malo
loq[ui] sicut eth        14 Si  b enim dimise
ni[ci] pu[ta]nt enim        ritis homini
quod [in]multi              bus peccata eo
loquio suo au               rum dimittet
diantur a                   uobis pater ues
```

C. 6.   Euangelium secundum Matthaeum.   7

temptationem, sed libera nos a malo. 14. Si enim dimiseritis hominibus peccata eorum, dimittet uobis et pater uester qui est in caelis. 15. Si autem non remiseritis hominibus peccata, nec pater uester remittet uobis peccata uestra. 16. Cum autem ieiunatis, nolite fieri sicut hypocritae tristes. Exterminant enim facies suas, ut appareant hominibus ieiunantes. Amen dico uobis: habent mercedem suam. 17. Uos autem cum ieiunatis, unguite caput uestrum, et faciem uestram lauate, 18. ne pareatis hominibus ieiunantes, sed patri uestro, qui est in absconso, et pater uester, qui uidet in absconso, reddet uobis

Codex Veronensis : ca. AD 450

The Aland Greek NT committee noted, in leaving these words out of their definitive text, that they were omitted in codex Sinaiticus, Vaticanus and codex Bezae, as well as virtually all the Old Latin versions of the New Testament. However, they are included in some of the other valuable manuscripts, such codex Alexandrinos, and the Ephraem Syrii text.

Moreover, there is a very important 'witness' to these words being what we could call "authentic", and that is the so-called 'Didache' or '*The Teachings of the 12 Apostles*'. In this text, the doxology is included at the end of the Prayer, although slightly abridged. As we noted earlier, this very valuable document is from the first century.

But what does 'authentic' mean? To mainstream scholars, the doxology is seen as being created by devout early Christians to give a ritualistic quality to the prayer, for use in churches. I have no doubt that this conclusion is correct.

For this 'doxology' was probably not spoken by Jesus as he intoned this great Prayer to his disciples, in a high spiritual realm. But there is a deeper aspect to these words, as revealed in brief comments from Rudolf Steiner, in a lecture from 1906. There he comments to the effect that these words derive from esoterically aware Christians, that is, those who were on an initiatory quest.

The ancient Coptic *Pistis Sophia* codex reveals the existence of a substantial initiatory schooling process being undertaken amongst some of the disciples of Christ. From Rudolf Steiner's words one can deduce that the doxology has validity; being a meditation upon the cycles of evolution that humanity has undergone and is undergoing.

The sequence of these words should be "For Thine is the Power, the Kingdom and the Glory". And this is the sequence in the earliest version ever found – that is the Didache, except that 'kingdom' is left out. It is common to find one of these three words left out in the various ancient manuscripts that record them.

Rudolf Steiner explains these terms in the context of the vast seven-fold cycles of evolution that humanity has undergone. He describes these epochs in his foundational book, *An Outline of Esoteric Science*; this cosmology is explained comprehensively, with diagrams, in my *Rudolf Steiner Handbook*.

In this context;
'Power' refers to the Aeons
'Kingdom' to the Cycles within the Aeons
and 'Glory' to the Phases within the Cycles

But now we must note that the esoterically informed Christian has to conclude that the deity who is revered in these words is not the cosmic Christ (who can also be called the Solar Logos); but is the primal Logos, who exists in the triune Godhead. This is because the cosmic Christ, the leader of the Powers (or Sun-gods), is not the Regent of the successive Aeons. These vast evolutionary epochs are governed by the primal Logos.

However, it is a profound truth which is a potent theme to meditate upon, that the primal Logos is present within the cosmic Christ. This profoundly exalted, twofold cosmic reality may not have been clear to those very early esoteric Christians who were inspired to compose this doxology.

Or perhaps they were indeed aware of this immensely deep and sacred truth of the 'interweaving' of the two deities, but would not have discussed it openly in written form. That is, that the sublime primal Logos was present within the cosmic Christ, the solar Logos. This is a theme which I discuss in my *The Gospel of John*, and *Rudolf Steiner on Leonardo's Last Supper*.

The original Aramaic text

There is some confusion about the Prayer being more powerful spiritually, if it is spoken in the ancient Aramaic language. Rudolf Steiner has commented on this topic, saying that if it were spoken in ancient Greek, then it would have more spiritual power than if spoken in a modern translation; but even more power if spoken in Aramaic. This is true for anyone just hearing it as a member of a group. The inner quality of the vowels and consonants have an impact on the listener, conveying a meaning which transcends logical understanding.

But to hear it as a part of a meditative intoning, as a specific meditative exercise, would be much more powerful if the devout Christian has been immersed in the Gospels.

However, such an exercise does not appear possible today, as the original wording of the prayer in Aramaic is unknown. Some people have thought that the Prayer, as found in the Peshitta Bible, which is written in Aramaic, gives us that possibility. But the Peshitta Bible is a translation into Aramaic from the Greek, and was made about 300 years after Jesus lived. Also, there are several ways into which any sentence can be translated into any another language.

But in addition, the mysterious word 'epiousion' was a riddle to the Greek-speaking Christians, and so it was translated incorrectly into Aramaic as bread 'for our needs', or as 'our daily bread'. What 'epiousion' would be in Aramaic is unknown.

But to contemplate the Lord's Prayer in an esoterically sensitive translation, with intuitive insight, with the understanding this yields as it resonates in your own mind, and thereby transcending intellectual assessment, is also very valuable to the soul.

It is this understanding based on initiatory insights, which makes the deeper meaning of the Greek text more perceptible. This is a modern way to develop a deeply living, inner link between one's soul and the sublime truths which the Christ has proclaimed in this Prayer.

APPENDIX ONE

That the 'i' can be left in the word epiousion

As we noted earlier, back in the fourth century, the great scholar Jerome concluded that it meant 'above material substance' (which is in Latin: *supersubstantialis*). And in the 19th century, before the research of Carmignac, some very highly respected scholars did acknowledge, if reluctantly, that 'epiousion' can indeed be a word coined from joining epi and ousia. In the 19th century, Bishop Lightfoot comments, "it would then mean: 'conducive to the 'ousia', i.e., the essential being (of the human). Lightfoot then concluded that the word means 'sufficient to sustain us'.[74]

Also in the 19th century, amidst the widespread dismissal of this understanding of the word, another brilliant Church of England scholar, Prof. Rev. Edward H. Plumptre, Dean of Wells, declared that indeed 'epi' and 'ousios' can be, and were, united by the Gospel writer to form this word; which means 'over and above material substance'.[75]

Plumptre was a highly skilled scholar; he not only worked with NT Greek but also with Classical Greek, translating the dramas of ancient Greece tragedians such as Aeschylos. In addition, he translated Dante's poem 'Divine Comedy' from Latin. (He was also an advocate for the advancement of women in the clergy.)

In the late 19th century, in French-speaking Alsace, the brilliant scholar Friedrich Godet also showed that this objection was without foundation. He quoted various ancient Greek words which

---

[74] Plumptre, *The Gospel according to St. Matthew*, p. 81, Cassell & Co. London, undated.
[75] Cited by J. Broadus, in *Commentary on Matthew*, p. 137

retained the 'i' even though this is ungrammatical.⁷⁶

In the 20th century, the eminent authority, Prof. Moulton concurred with Plumptre, writing, "...so Jerome's *supersubstantialis* is not finally discredited by the non-removal of the 'i' ".⁷⁷ As noted above, in antiquity, Origenes and Jerome-Hieronymous accepted the validity of this word, but they were not sure as to what it meant.

I concur with Origenes and others after him, that this word seems to have been artificially created by the Gospel writer. In addition, through being so odd, in that it retains the 'i', this word is designed to be seen as directly contrasting with another word, 'periousion', which means 'surplus, or 'abundance'.

---

⁷⁶ F.Godet, Kommentar zu dem Evangelium des Lukas, p. 354.
⁷⁷ J.H. Moulton, *Grammar of the NT Grk.* vol.2, p.313.

APPENDIX TWO

The various words formed from MHR

(The hyphen used in the first downwards row, is intended to indicate a pause was made before speaking the next letter.)

1 māhâ-r (מָהַר)   = to flow on/ run on/ be in motion

2 māhā-r (מָהָר)   = morning, tomorrow, or a futural event

3 māho-r (מַהֵר)   = hastily, quickly

4 māhâ-r (מָהַר)   = to exchange, or to offer up (to something)

(The same verb as #1, but in a different condition[78])

5 mohr (מָהַר)   = to offer up (to something) and also: to immerse/ let pour into/ exchange for/ let flow into

6 mo-hâr (מֹהַר)   = a dowry

(Here a noun, but as an adjective, this word means, 'given-over' or 'offering up' of something which is valued, to someone else)

Fürst concluded that the word maho-r also gave rise to:
nāmâ-r (נָמַר) = transforms itself/ metamorphoses itself

---

[78] Technically, the first condition of the verb is 'transitive', but this second condition is 'intransitive'.

APPENDIX 3

Three other versions of this key sentence are:

"Transmigration comes to an end with the advent of the Christ, and faith is preached for the forgiveness of sins..." D. Litwa, p. 591

"But by the instrumentality of the Saviour, the transference of soul (from) body to body ceases, and faith is preached for the remission of sins."
J. H. MacMahon, p. 217

"Since the time of the Saviour, transmigration ceased; faith is proclaimed for the forgiveness of sins" (Seit des Heilands Zeit hat die Seelenwanderung aufgehört, der Glaube wird verkündet zur Vergebung der Sünden.)
Graf von Preysing, p. 153

My version again is:

"Then, because of the Saviour, **discussing ceases of reincarnation**, and so Faith is preached (*instead*) concerning the release from sins."

The situation here is that verb used (pauoe - παύω) not only means 'to cease, 'to stop', but also specifically 'to stop talking', or 'to stop singing' – without 'singing' or 'speaking' being written down. The singing or speaking can be referred to one or two lines earlier.

It was used this way for example, by Homer in *The Odyssey*, (Bk. 17; lines 345-360), where Odysseus in disguise enters the great hall of his home,
"Then he sat down...and ate so long as the minstrel sang in the halls. But when he had dined and the divine minstrel ceased playing, the suitors broke into uproar..."[79]

---

[79] In Homer's Grk. "the divine minstrel ceased playing: ὁ δ' ἀπαυετο θεῖος αοιδος ".

Even though the reference to the minstrel's singing was in the line before, the verb 'pauoe' here means 'to cease singing', not to simply 'cease'.[80]

Since the Doketai text that Hippolytos refers to, has a substantial reference to reincarnation some lines earlier, I conclude that the verb 'pauoe' used here also is referring back to discussing reincarnation.

If the first part of the sentence meant 'with the Saviour, reincarnation ceases', then not only is this absurd, but it is also disconnected from the second part of the sentence: "Therefore, Faith is preached (*instead*) concerning the cancelling of sins".

It is disconnected, because to the Doketai there is no meaningful link between all humanity ceasing to reincarnate, and the preaching of faith. For to them, such a preaching method would not achieve what many life-times can – the erasure of the lower self or 'sinfulness' from the soul-body.

Here I need to note that the word 'therefore' is not used in the other versions; instead they have 'and' or they ignore the word 'therefore' and just use a comma: "...and faith is preached for the forgiveness of sins". In the German version there is only a comma: "...transmigration ceased, faith is proclaimed for the forgiveness of sins".

Now the little Greek word, translated by me as 'therefore' and joining these two parts of the sentence is 'te', which can indeed simply mean 'and', as these other scholars have interpreted it.

---

[80] The ancient historian Herodotus also used the verb in this way (*Histories*, Bk. 7:8d).

But its especial meaning is 'and so' or 'so'; or 'therefore/consequently'.[81]

An examination of how Hippolytus uses 'te' reveals that he does not use it to mean 'and', but to mean 'and so' and by implication, 'thus/therefore'.

Here are some examples, which are translated by others as 'and' – but where Hippolytus presents a situation and then is presenting a conclusion about a specific matter'; so here 'and' fails to present his meaning.

Book 6: Simon and Helen.
"Now the prophets inspired by spirit-messengers who made the world, spoke their prophecies. For this reason, those who believe in Simon and Helen do not give any consideration to them. Consequently (*te*) they busy themselves, as 'free' persons, however they wish."[82]

If the *te* is ignored, and starts with "they busy..." the sentence loses its relation to the sentence before.

Book 8 : Allegory of the Passover
"The number One (*i.e., the Monad*) up the number 4 contained in the number 14 .... is the perfect number (*i.e., ten*). And so (*te*) indeed, the one + two + three + four makes 10."[83]

If the *te* is omitted, or understood as 'and', then the reference of the concluding sentence to the preceding sentence is lost.

---

[81] This is because technically it is in Greek grammar an 'enclitic particle' and often serves to join together two statements by showing that they are interrelated.

[82] In Grk. "...πράσσειν τε ὅσα βούλονται ὡς ἐλευθέρους .

[83] In Grk. " τό τε γὰρ ἕν, δύο, τριά,τέσσαρα γίνεται δέχα ..."

The word 'te' also has this core meaning in a brief obscure meditative text; where it does not mean 'and' and has to be included:

Book 8: Monoimos
 "Ocean: and thus (*te*) birth of Gods,
 and thus (*te*) birth of human beings"[84]

But most significantly, there are also numerous passages where both 'and' (*kai*) as well as 'and so' (*te*) occur in the same sentence, next to each other; showing that to Hippolytos '*te*' does not mean 'and':

Book 8: Phrygians
"I…. have proved that the majority of their books are absurd, so and (*te kai*) all their arguments are weak and not worthy of consideration.."[85]

Book 7: Basileides
":…The Great Ruler ….is head of the world. A (spirit-)power who cannot be described as beautiful, and so (*te kai*), in general not as great and powerful…"[86]

These examples show us that the common translation,

"Then, because of the Saviour, reincarnation ceases, **and** Faith is preached concerning the forgiving of sins"

is not helpful. The first part of the sentence is implausible regarding the Doketai, and the over-all sentence would be illogical to the Doketai.

---

[84] In Grk. " Ὠκεανός γένεσίς τε Θειῶν γένεσίς τ' ἀνθρώπων.
[85] In Grk. "… αὐτῶν βιβλία τε καὶ (ἐ)πιξειπήματα πᾶσιν ἀσθενῆ…"
[86] In Grk .. ἡ κεφαλὴ τοῦ κόσμου κάλλος τε καὶ μέγεθος ἡ δύναμις.

Moreover the second part is inaccurate to how Hippolytos used 'te'.

A third point of grammar needs to be briefly mentioned. In my translation:
"Then, because of the Saviour, **discussion ceases of reincarnation**, therefore Faith is preached (*instead*) concerning the release from sins" –
the phrase 'of reincarnation' can be viewed by students of ancient Greek as incorrect to the Greek, as the word 'of' is missing in the Greek.

Indeed it should be there, but as scholars are aware, this 'genitive' case of the noun is quite often neglected by Greeks, (especially with the 'Genitive Absolute'), including in the New Testament. It is entirely valid to view the word 'reincarnation' as meaning 'of reincarnation' (see the foot-note for the technical aspect of this).[87]

The Greek of this sentence in Hippolytos:

ἀπό δὲ σωτῆρος μετενσωμάτωσις πέπαυται πίστις τε κηρύσσεται εἰς ἄφεσιν ἁμαρτιῶν ....

---

[87] "of reincarnation": this is a possessive case, yet the noun is in the nominative case. That a noun has not been placed in the genitive case is an error of which quite a few examples exist in the NT, known as a 'Nominativus Pendens. Such a glitch is in effect an anacoluthon; in this case, a substantive at the head of a clause without construction. That a noun remains in the nomin. case but should be in the gen. case is especially found with the Genitive Absolute situation (e.g., in Matt.1:18).

Books by this Author

Living a Spiritual Year: seasonal festivals in both hemispheres (new, expanded edition, 2016)	1992
The Way to the Sacred	2003
The Foundation Stone Meditation: a new commentary	2005
Dramatic Anthroposophy: Identification and contextualization of primary features of Rudolf Steiner's anthroposophy. (PhD thesis)	2005
Two Gems from Rudolf Steiner	2014
The Hellenistic Mysteries & Christianity	2014
Rudolf Steiner Handbook	2014
Horoscope Handbook – a Rudolf Steiner Approach	2015
The Meaning of the Goetheanum Windows	2016
The Lost Zodiac of Rudolf Steiner	2016
Rudolf Steiner's Esoteric Christianity in the Grail painting by Anna May	2017
The Vidar Flame Column – its meaning from Rudolf Steiner	2017
Rudolf Steiner on Leonardo's *Last Supper*	2017
Rudolf Steiner's First Class Verses	2018
Blessed - Rudolf Steiner on the Beatitudes	2018
The Soul's Calendar - annotated with Commentary	2019
The Soul's Calendar - pocket edition	2019
The Apocalyptic Seals from Rudolf Steiner	2020

The Mysteries of Ephesos	2021
The Gospel of John; an Initiatory Pathway Translation & Commentary	2022
Pistis Sophia: the ancient Coptic codex in a new translation and Commentary	2024

Also, under the pen-name Damien Pryor:

The nature & origin of the Tropical Zodiac	2011
Stonehenge	2011
Lalibela	2011
The Externsteine	2011
The Great Pyramid & the Sphinx	2011

www.ingramcontent.com/pod-product-compliance
Lightning Source LLC
Chambersburg PA
CBHW060837170426
43192CB00019BA/2810